CREATING YOUR FIRST EVER CV

IN SEVEN EASY STEPS

Other study skills titles from How To Books:

THE COMPLETE STUDY SKILLS GUIDE
A practical guide for all students who want to know how to learn
Dr Catherine Dawson

WRITING A UCAS PERSONAL STATEMENT IN SEVEN EASY STEPS
*A really useful guide to creating a
successful personal statement*
Julia Dolowicz

HOW TO PASS YOUR EXAMS
Proven techniques for any exam that will guarantee success
Mike Evans

THE JOY OF ENGLISH
100 Illuminating conversations about the English language
Jesse Karjalainen

HOW TO PASS PSYCHOMETRIC TESTS
*This book gives you information, confidence
and plenty of practice*
Andrea Shavick

Write or phone for a catalogue to:

How To Books
Spring Hill House
Spring Hill Road
Begbroke
Oxford
OX5 1RX
Tel. 01865 375794

Or email: info@howtobooks.co.uk

Visit our website www.howtobooks.co.uk to find out more
about us and our books.

Like our Facebook page How To Books & Spring Hill

Follow us on Twitter @Howtobooksltd

Read our books online www.howto.co.uk

CREATING YOUR FIRST EVER CV

IN SEVEN EASY STEPS

HOW TO BUILD A WINNING SKILLS-BASED CV FOR THE VERY FIRST TIME

JULIA DOLOWICZ

howtobooks

This book is dedicated to my Mum and Dad, who have always been 'right behind me'. They have shown enthusiasm, pride and joy in all that I do and have done, while being supportive through difficult times. They have been, and continue to be, wonderful parents.

This book is for you.

Northamptonshire Libraries & Information Services NC		
Askews & Holts		

Published by How To Books Ltd,
Spring Hill House, Spring Hill Road,
Begbroke, Oxford OX5 1RX, United
Tel: (01865) 375794 Fax: (01865) 379
info@howtobooks.co.uk
www.howtobooks.co.uk

How To Books greatly reduce the carbon footprint of their books by sourcing their typesetting and printing in the UK.

British Library Cataloguing in Publication Data.
A catalogue record for this book is available from the British Library.

ISBN 978 1 84528 496 1

Produced for How To Books by Deer Park Productions, Tavistock
Typeset by PDQ Typesetting, Newcastle-under-Lyme, Staffordshire
Printed and bound in Great Britain by Bell & Bain Ltd, Glasgow

NOTE: The material contained in this book is set out in good faith for general guidance and no liability can be accepted for loss or expense incurred as a result of relying in particular circumstances on statements made in the book. The laws and regulations are complex and liable to change, and readers should check the current position with the relevant authorities before making personal arrangements.

Contents

Part Three   Interviews: You've Got One!

Part Four   Hints from Employers and Frequently Asked Questions (FAQs)

Recommendations from clients

'Julia's work is truly inspirational. She understands what employers are looking for in successful candidates and can translate this to offer advice and guidance to job seekers. She can help candidates identify and articulate their skills enabling them to maximise their chances of success in a very competitive labour market. Her contribution is invaluable.' *Colette Ashbrook, Graduate Accelerator Programme Manager, Liverpool John Moores University*

'While I was at university the thought of applying for jobs seemed over-whelming. Julia helped me to realise my career path and update my CV. She helped me identify skills I forgot I had. I am really proud of my CV and feel so much more confident about my future. The whole experience reached above and beyond my expectations.' *Rachael Ansar, BA (Philosophy and Ethics)*

'I contacted Julia after a friend told me that she would get me started on writing a personal statement for my university application. After we "met" over Skype, I felt confident to start writing it. She gave helpful hints and made me think of things about my skills. I was accepted to the university of my choice with an unconditional offer thanks to Julia.' *Michal Kramer, London, BSc Radiography (Radiotherapy and Oncology)*

'Having seen Julia work with students of all ages, I was deeply impressed by her ability to communicate with them on various levels and instill in them an infectious enthusiasm for university life and selling their skills on paper. I could not think of a better person who would be suited to critiquing personal statements or coaching you to create your first ever CV – using the enormous amount of knowledge she has, she enables individuals to make the most out of their application or CV.' *Simon Hackett, BSc, MSC, DPhil candidate Dunn School of Pathology, University of Oxford, Oxford.*

'Julia is a natural trainer, able to impart knowledge and facilitate exercises in a way that encourages reflection and learning. She is full of integrity and has a very personable approach to working with both colleagues and clients. Along with excellent coaching, training and development skills, I wholeheartedly recommend her to any training organisation or client and I hope that you enjoy working with her as much as I have.' *Sally Beyer, Learning and Development Consultant.*

Acknowledgements

This book couldn't have happened without the help and love from my husband William, who gave me the space to write and helped me balance my time in front of the laptop. I am also incredibly lucky to have a husband who enjoys cooking vegetarian food! Once again I couldn't have written this without my constant four-legged companion, Lucy, who reminded me to step away from the screen and get out into nature, while providing necessary hugs in between.

Much of the information in this book has been gathered from my time working with private clients and one-to-one mentoring sessions with young people at Liverpool College, so thank you to them for providing questions and insight to their experiences. Marking self-awareness statements for Liverpool John Moores University's World of Work programme has also given me an opportunity to delve into how individuals express themselves on paper, helping me to formulate and fine-tune my ideas and my process, while developing this writing practice.

I haven't been the most sociable creature these past few months as I have entered the writing phase, so thank you to close friends who understood that it was just what I needed to do. There were episodes of thinking I couldn't fit everything in, so thank you to Gaille for talking me through and realising that this was exactly what I had been working towards. I also want to thank Dr Sacha for his feedback and help.

It was Nikki Read from How to Books Ltd who approached me and suggested that I think about writing this book. So thank you, Nikki, for putting that thought out there and for, once again, publishing my words.

Preface

While working with young people as a careers coach, helping them to figure out their next step and supporting them through their challenges, I recognised that when they asked me about how to write their first ever CV, I would take them through the process that I am going to share with you in this book. What is often a really daunting task – selling yourself on the page – can be introduced in a very creative way so that you can transform the skills that you have accumulated to produce a workable CV that will hopefully secure a part-/full-time job, a voluntary opportunity, or some work experience. This book will therefore relate to you if you have never created a CV.

I am always seeking out books that I can add to the library and yet I find there are few books that relate to starting from scratch. Yes, there are a handful of books geared to the first timer, but greater quantities of the titles out there are geared to developing your CV further, for undergraduates, postgraduates and professionals. Contained in this mix is a selection of small handbooks that are put together by schools, careers services and specialised companies, including online information, which tend to be focused on how to build a chronological CV, with little or no discussion about integrating skills and strengths into it.

I don't sit in this camp.

From where I sit, young people, who don't necessarily have an employment history, can still enthuse about, declare and portray the strengths and skills they have gained from their life into a CV document, the difference being that their reference point might start from their school life and local community. This is known as your 'frame of reference'.

The same would be true if you were creating your CV having just been in one job since leaving school (and you were fortunate to secure this without a CV). Your 'frame of reference' will be based around the experiences you have gleaned from your first job, previous educational experience and local community involvements. Let's not forget the international community, now that the majority of people are online and interacting with forums, blogs and sites all over the world.

Consequently, the key is to combine a timeline of education and work experience, which speaks for itself, alongside skill groups that *you choose* in order to summarise your strengths, abilities, traits, and experience. In this format, you'll be selling yourself – totally. Your CV will express the experiences you have had. They might not be in a work environment, but they still highlight your characteristics, uniqueness, personality and individuality.

That's all that you can aim to achieve.

If you can capture these traits and provide evidence to show and prove your distinctiveness, then you will shine to a potential employer.

Whoever reads your finished CV, whether they are an employer for full-time or part-time work, an organisation or a charity for voluntary placement, or even a short stint of ad hoc shadowing, you will be able to capture their attention. What you believe are your strengths can be supported by examples of how you can help support their small business, company or organisation.

As a result, in thinking all this through, I then began to break down the seven steps I introduce to my students into a recognisable formula, so that you too can follow it. *Let it be known that this is a creative journey and not just about tran- scribing educational achievements onto a piece of paper.* You have to dig deep and reflect on your own *self*, asking others for their thoughts too. You will finally achieve a document that you will be very proud to show to others – one that sums you up in a great way.

The CV market is awash with templates. I'm not going to focus on the template but I'm going to help you discover your own strengths and skills, revealing aspects about your life and experiences to date.

Templates are great, but you have to know what to put in them, right?

You can always fit a template around the writing. It's difficult to do it the other way round.

So this is aimed at you. You're starting from scratch. You might have a few lines of qualifications and contact details written somewhere on a Word document, hidden in the depths of your computer. But that's about it.

I sincerely hope that you find this book a creative approach to building your CV and that you surprise yourself with who you are and what you have to offer. Wishing you the very best of luck as you progress.

Julia Dolowicz
Liverpool
www.juliadolowicz.com

Foreword

There are many strange and remarkable elements of our education system but nothing is more remarkable than how much energy and time is spent by students, counsellors and trainers learning and developing skills which are never made clear or communicated to any prospective employer. We spend hours, days, and even years learning things but only minutes developing a strategy and document to make sure that what we know, have learned and can do is communicated clearly and effectively to prospective employers.

The result, of course is frustration. An entire generation of young people is unable to bring all its talents and skills to bear on a competitive and global job market. Many never have the opportunity to use their skills or develop and apply what they have learned.

Julia Dolowicz has done every job applicant a huge favour by writing this practical, common-sense approach to creating a CV for the very first time. Schools and universities, for the most part, fail in their task of teaching students how to create a CV, which explains not only what they have done but also what they can do. Like a good CV, this book delivers its message, in part, through its own form. It is concise, practical and to the point.

Most applicants use a template to write a CV. The results are documents that tend to be too long, focused too much on qualifications and far too little on what the prospective employee can do for the prospective employer.

Ms Dolowicz's experience as a counsellor, careers coach and author have all contributed to the usefulness of this innovative book which is certain to help men and women get the jobs that challenge and inspire them.

Hans van Mourik Broekman

Principal

Liverpool College

HMC Independent IB World School for girls and boys aged 3-18

Introduction

Does this sound like you?

First things first, it's important that you're here because you are creating your first ever CV. Before you go any further, does this sound like you?

- You're currently still in school and want to apply for work experience.

- You're currently in school/college and want to find a part-time job – everyone keeps asking you to email your CV. You don't have one and you have no clue where to begin.

- You're thinking of leaving school after GCSEs and want to get a job.

- You're considering that, after sixth form and/or college, you don't want to go to university, but want to find a job.

- You want to find and apply for an apprenticeship that you will love.

- You have a job, which you've had for a while, you got it through someone you knew and you now want to 'move on' to another job. You don't have any support with this.

- You have been out of the job market for many years, your CV is pretty outdated and you don't know how to sell your strengths and skills.

- You are about to leave the services; you have a CV related to your service career but you are beginning to search for jobs. Ideally, you want help in profiling your strengths and skills in a very positive way and ultimately want to find out how to transfer them to a civvy CV.

Familiarise yourself with terminology included in the book

CV	Curriculum vitae – (meaning 'courses of life')
Chronological	A record of events starting with the earliest and following the order in which they occurred
Criteria	Standards for judging things
Employee specification	This is a list of criteria, which records what the employer is seeking. It is often broken down into: Essential criteria (necessary) Desirable criteria (wanted, advantageous)
Job description	Describing the actual role of the job
Speculative	Exploratory. Often we send speculative CVs or letters to introduce ourselves to an employer when there isn't necessarily a job being advertised
Profile	An outline, summary or overview of our strengths, experiences, skills and interests. Usually placed at the beginning of a CV

CVs, being employable and the job market

It can be difficult to create a CV when you have never attempted one before. It's even more difficult when you have little or no work history to show. We are often told to create one, because 'everyone does'. The art of devising a CV is more about the research you do beforehand and the types of jobs you are seeking. The day has gone of 'one size fits all' or having a single CV to send to countless people. In this competitive environment, it's just not viable.

Of course there are facts and information about you that a potential recruiter will want to read and this has pretty much stayed the same for a long while. Things such as:

- contact information;
- education;
- qualifications;
- work history/experience;
- relevant skills;
- personal interests;
- references.

For many years, CVs just contained this information and nothing more. It was almost a list – in order of time, so that recruiters could review where you'd been and what you'd done.

CVs have morphed into various formats. I'm not going to bombard you with all the differences; instead, I will give you an overview of the different types of CVs and how that is going to be relevant to us, here and now.

Types of CVs

CVs can be written in a number of ways and for this seven-step process, I am going to be combining chronological and skills-based CVs. I also want to share with you the whole new idea of interactive CVs – these could also become more available in the recruitment process, especially in these technological years.

Chronological CV

In a nutshell, this means 'an order of time'. CVs written in this way are a record of events starting with the earliest and following the order in which they occurred. They will show any potential recruiter what you have done, featuring headings such as education, qualifications and employment history. These will always be listed in date order, starting from the most recent and working backwards.

If you're starting to write your CV with not much of an employment story to tell, then using only this type of CV might mean that the page may look 'spacey'. Too many 'white bits' and not enough to show and tell.

Using an entirely chronological format, you'll probably find that you will have one page of A4. With limited or no work history this could be you.

Does this sell your experiences and skills? Do you want to express yourself more?

Skills-based CV

You choose your five or six top skill categories and provide a specific example, which highlights this skill, enabling a future employer to see your proof, straight away. Skill categories can be for example: Communication – speaking; Communication – presenting; Organisation and planning; IT and media skills; Using initiative and solving problems.

A skills-based CV can be really helpful if it is your first ever CV and of course, combined with a chronology, it can prove to be an interesting read. When writing a CV that is based on your skills, you will be able to sell yourself more favourably. Often you have had many experiences throughout school, college or community and maybe also your first job. Therefore, you need to organise these strengths.

CVIV interactive video

Interactive CVs are becoming more popular. These are visual and often stored online via YouTube and Vimeo. If you're aiming to get a job within a creative industry, it is more acceptable to be creative and develop a mini film, which incorporates different aspects of your strengths and profiles your skill set to a very high standard (that's if it is produced well, of course). An interactive CV is still a new adventure, but there are definitely more opportunities to provide an interactive CV along with a written CV.

The job market is changing and the types of jobs available are reflecting this interactive age. Will the jobs of today be available in the next ten years? Will we have a whole new realm of jobs? Thinking how prevalent Facebook, Twitter, YouTube and the interactive/gaming industries are, we might find that interactive CVs will become more acceptable.

For now, you have to use your initiative when creating an interactive CV but you'll probably find that employers will still want to see a hard copy of a CV as well.

An example of a similar type of interactive CV that became worldwide and well known happened about three years ago when Tourism Queensland asked for a 60-second video explanation to be submitted as an application for 'the post of caretaker on Hamilton Island in the Great Barrier Reef'. This was combined with the usual filling out of an online application form.

It was a six-month contract, with flexible working hours and the successful candidate's 'key responsibilities' included exploring the area to discover what was on offer and to report back weekly via blogs, photo diaries, video updates and media interviews.

They received thousands of video applications as the job went viral and after all the shortlisting, the job was awarded to Brit Ben Southall. If you want to see this you can view his video application on YouTube. This job advertisement was unique and grabbed the attention of thousands of people (http://www.you tube.com/watch?v=PnosVJfDrpY).

New tools, many of them related to the explosion in use of social media, are transforming the recruitment world. The way the job went viral was pretty phenomenal. Many individuals applied and it shows us that employers are looking outside the box when it comes to recruiting. Of course, this job on Hamilton Island lent itself to this creative application process, but it is worth bearing in mind that this may feature somewhere along the line.

If you're a creative spark, you may find this could be another string to your bow. It adds to the new breed of job seeker. If you spend time developing an interactive CV, make sure the production and editing are seamless and good quality. With the equipment available these days, it's entirely possible to do this yourself.

Another example of a CVIV (a curriculum vitae interactive video) is that of Graeme Anthony, who needed to get a new job in PR in a hurry when he moved from Manchester to London. His YouTube video is simple yet effective (http://www.youtube.com/watch?feature=player_embedded&v=9EzNll1U2N8).

In this video, Anthony sits behind a table pitching his skills and then links appear to more videos giving greater detail. 'It brings me to life in a completely new way,' he explains. 'It shows off my personality in a way a paper CV can't.'

It worked. When a London PR agency saw the video, Graeme was quickly invited for an interview, and got the job.

It is amazing that in this day and age, more candidates don't resort to these kinds of hi-tech CVs and it is also amazing that, as things have moved so quickly from a technological point of view, CVs are still the same as they were 10, 15 or even 20 years ago.

This book is not about developing an interactive CV but this type of approach certainly needs mentioning.

YouTube throws up plenty of examples of the new breed of job-seeker, promoting themselves with video offerings.

Social networking for first-time job hunters

Social networking is becoming integrated into the recruitment process. There are positive aspects to using social media. LinkedIn is all about professional rather than personal lives and it has become the place where jobseekers come to display their wares and employers check out their credentials.

Getting your social networking profile in order is vital. That means making sure your visible profile on Facebook is suitable. You may have potential employers viewing it.

Your profile – what is it?

You've heard people mentioning the term 'profile' and you certainly know what a profile is in terms of social media. However in the CV context, a profile can be known as a 'statement', a 'summary' or an 'overview'. It is a short paragraph that starts off your CV and summarises key strengths, skills, abilities, characteristics and traits that you would like a potential recruiter to view – and view it quickly. When employers read your CV very quickly they will often read your profile first.

Your profile is something that you will compile in Step Four, when your CV is becoming more solid. By then, you will have a clear overview of your skill categories and evidence and you will begin to choose what elements you would like to include. I have read many profiles/summaries/statements. They need to sound punchy so it's best not to write them first but towards the end when you have so much more awareness about yourself, about the jobs you're considering and about the way to formulate your words.

The skill in writing your profile is to avoid the 'itsy bitsy' words that we would add into a sentence; for example; 'I have', 'I am', 'the', 'and', 'in', 'of', 'at'. This we will look at later on, so don't worry about it just now. Don't expect to know how to write the profile at this beginning stage. It will all unfold in its own good time.

A step-by-step overview

Before you begin the seven steps, I want to explain more about the actual stages, so I have created an overview. My aim for this book is for you to drop in and complete activities whenever you have time. You don't have to complete all of it in order; however, it will make more sense as I introduce to you different topics about building your CV.

It's up to you.

Step One – Gather It

This step is all about collecting the material to start creating your 'principal CV'. Here you will be introduced to the idea of creating a profile, a short paragraph, about four or five lines at the top of your CV, which takes all your skills, abilities and dreams, and places them right at the beginning to catch the attention of a potential recruiter. It is a summary of who you are and is often the first thing an employer will read. The chapter will explain in more detail why having a principal CV is important and how it will feed into all your future CVs.

You will have activities to complete, starting with **Activity 1.1: Go get it**, where I ask you to begin to write down the kind of jobs you're seeking. Following this is **Activity 1.2: Go with the flow**, which asks you to involve five other people in your life so that you can begin to discover the skills/traits/abilities people see in you and therefore how you start to view yourself. **Activity 1.3: Start your time line**, encourages you to bring together information from your timeline, dates, times, addresses, telephone numbers, grades, all things relating to education, examinations, schooling and qualifications. To finish off this first step, in **Activity 1.4: Pruning**, you are asked to research further the types of jobs that are relevant to you and here I ask you to begin to collect information from jobs that are being advertised locally, nationally and globally in the newspapers and online.

Step Two – Develop It

We move now into a phase where you take all the information you have gathered and start to adapt it. By now you have collected your job adverts. You will be introduced to what a job description and employee/person specification look like and you will be asked to find this for jobs you're considering. You will choose three different jobs that are enticing you and discover all the relevant job information from them. If you haven't found a job, work experience or opportunity that you want – just choose. Go on. Dream. If you'd love to work for the Apple Store, then choose them, print off the job data for one of their roles. I will be taking you through a selection of activities that will help you find your skills and strengths. In **Activity 2.1: Craft a 'target job profile'** you will be shown how to pick out all the important words used in the job descriptions and employee specification, learning to notice the similarities between them. This activity will help to familiarise yourself with the terminology that they use to describe skills, strengths, abilities and attributes. You'll feel more confident about what they are seeking and the skills they are after.

In **Activity 2.2: Taking stock of strengths and skills** we are going to look at your skills in a little more detail to discover which ones you feel confident about and which ones you don't. You will find 78 questions split into 13 groups where you have to score yourself depending on how you feel about each written statement. In completing this activity you will hopefully begin to see where you feel confident about particular areas, detecting your strengths and weaknesses.

Next up is **Activity 2.3: Five chief skill categories** – you now have the chance to choose five skill categories you feel are your strongest and those where you have the most evidence to show to a potential employer/recruiter. You will begin to form headings, preparing the ground for giving examples. These five chief skills become the basis of your principal CV and highlight the overlap between what you have discovered in your 'target job profile' and the most prominent skill categories that you have found by doing 'taking stock of strengths and skills'.

Step Three – Prove It

Here you will begin to start thinking of specific examples where you have used a skill, a strength, shown initiative, or realised your potential. Using the **Activity 3.1: Reveal more**, I choose eight different categories for you and ask you to think of specific instances or occasions where you have done something like it. I will demonstrate by giving you an example of each one. This will begin to reveal where you exhibit ability and proficiency. Using the headings of Communication – speaking, Communication – listening; Organising; Working independently; Team work; Information technology; Using initiative and solving problems; and Specific talents, you will be beginning to prove how your potential has been realised.

The purpose of this activity is to get the ideas on the page. You will find employers are always on the look out for examples and evidence of the above categories. As this forms your Principal CV, you will be able to tweak the skills for the specific job you're after, at a later date. In **Activity 3.2: Skill surprise**, we take this further and you are asked to think of more examples and evidence that can show where you're excelling.

Step Four – Draft It

This step goes into detail of the shape our CV takes – the format, the style, the structure and the layout. In **Activity 4.1: Draw up your CV structure**, you will find a blank outline, where you start to pull together some of the evidence you have been collecting. We'll also discuss more about your Profile and what are you hoping to achieve with it. At this point, you will begin to outline your profile in **Activity 4.2**.

You may wonder why you are creating your profile in Step Four. Often we think that we can create our profile earlier on, when in fact, it's more difficult to do this because we haven't collected enough information about ourselves and about the companies where we want to apply. When we begin to build a picture of (a) what we're seeking, (b) what they're seeking, (c) what skills we have that we're good at and (d) what skills they want, we feel more confident to pitch to them. I use the term 'them'. You may not be applying right now for a job. But you have to have in your mind's eye an idea of where it is you wish to work. What industry? Retail, hospitality, games, computing, fashion or even your local corner shop.

> ## That's why you are building a picture of 'them'.
> ## To help you build a picture of 'you'.

This activity takes the words/skills that you discovered in **Activities 1.2, 2.1** and **2.3** and you start to create a small paragraph about six lines long.

Step Five – Build It

Here you'll be building even more, adapting the information you have gathered, developed, proved and drafted so far. Having made many notes in the previous steps in your notebook, you will now follow the format I provide and assemble your principal CV. You're going to begin to build it. In **Activity 5.1: Tweak your chief skills**, you will write examples for each of your chief skills, and I will show you how to remove the 'itsy-bitsy' words you have written in order to create evidence that sits snugly on one line, making your finished principal CV format look neat and selling your competencies beautifully.

In **Activity 5.2: Profile and evidence MOT**, you will find some descriptive and action words to help boost your profile or your evidence sentences. In this activity you will find a thorough list of 161 words; some will appeal, others won't. In this activity the idea is to circle any words that you think you could use to make your own sentences sound more professional and descriptive.

Step Six – Polish It

We're on the last stretch and by now you hopefully have quite a lot written down. You may be surprised by how much information you have collected. This next step is about adding, subtracting, reshaping and making things sound as if they make sense and noticing if you're repeating yourself. If you don't feel you have enough evidence for your five chief skills categories, then I suggest you go back and research the industries/companies in more detail. Find out what skills, attributes, knowledge, strengths, and characteristics they want. If you find you don't have enough, you could be underselling yourself and your skills. Perhaps you're not sure whom you're writing this CV for? Go back to Step One and dig some more.

In **Activity 6.1: Here come the hints** – I will illustrate what is acceptable and not acceptable in CVs and any written statement – things that relate to being too repetitive, being too general, using the word 'try', the word 'nice', direct quotes, humour, telling fibs, using colour and photographs. **Activity 6.2: 'Bring on' the feedback** – is a supportive write-up because I know you're itching to release your draft CV and profile for family, tutors and friends to review. It's important to hand it over to someone you feel will highlight the positives and negatives. At this stage, there is always room for a nip/tuck. You want someone who can pick up on spelling mistakes and any grammatical errors.

Step Seven – Complete It

Step Seven introduces you to the 4Rs: review, refine, rejig and reassure. Here, you are encouraged to review, refine and rejig your CV so that it reads and flows well. By this point you have a principal CV that is really selling your strengths and skills. We'll finish this section of the book with **Activity 7.1: Know your network,** which will get you thinking about people you may already know in your network and community.

In Part Two, I will be giving attention to how to write a covering letter, including how to set it out, what kind of information to include and just how important it is when a recruiter receives it. The main aim of a covering letter is to compile one that takes information from your profile and CV and builds it into a great introduction letter.

In Part Three, you may be wondering 'what if I get an interview?' I say, 'Well done!' Here, I advise you how to prepare for it the best way possible.

I will also share how to complete application forms and a brief overview about expression statements. Part Four contains some hints from real employers in my circle. These people read CVs, application forms and covering letters from individuals who don't have a long work history, offering work experiences, opportunities, shadowing, part-time as well as full-time work. Any tips that they share, I will pass on to you. I will also include frequently asked questions (FAQs) that I have been asked over time.

There's much to get through. If you seriously want to create your CV from scratch, then this book will take you through that process, building a winning skills-based CV that will give you an opportunity to first know what your skills and strengths are and, second, promote them on paper.

It's all good stuff. Let the party commence.

Part One
Creating Your First Ever CV in Seven Easy Steps

Step One

Gather It

This first phase is where you are going to begin to collect and assemble information about yourself, including the data you'll need to include in your CV. On top of this you'll also start bringing together advertisements of jobs that are appealing to you. They may be examples of jobs that you have seen in the past, or are current jobs where you intend to submit your CV. You may also research any information sheets about voluntary work in your community, or specific shadowing opportunity that you wish to obtain.

That's why I call this section 'Gather it', as you will bring all the relevant bits of information about yourself into one place. There are a few activities where you will have the opportunity to ask people you know about your skills and, subsequently, begin to build a picture of what you're projecting into the world, recognising what you're good at and noticing what people see about you.

Your principal CV and profile

In this step I'm going to introduce you to what I call your principal CV which will include a profile to sit at the top of your CV. To recap, a profile is a summary of *who you are* and is often *the first thing* that an employer reads about you. It takes all your skills, abilities and dreams, and places them right at the top in order to catch the attention of a potential recruiter. This chapter will explain in more detail why having a principal CV is important and how it will feed into all your future CVs and any written letters that you compile.

Why aren't we just starting to write our CV straight away?

From my experience working with people, devising CVs, writing personal statements for jobs, university and completing application forms, it is so much more difficult to write a CV when you don't have any idea of the end goal. It makes the task of beginning very laborious, when it really doesn't have to be. The hardest part of starting is feeling unsure whom you're writing your CV for – is it for a specific job that you know is being advertised, or are you planning to send some out speculatively and pitch for work? Are you seeking a placement or are you looking for some work experience? Are you registering with agencies? Is sending a CV a requirement? Have you thought about any of this yet?

Once you've decided who is going to receive your very first CV, it becomes a little easier as you will gather information from them and you will begin to formulate an overview of who will be reading your CV and, more importantly, what skills they require.

This may not be the exact job you'll be using your CV for, however, when you identify what a similar job role requires. Even if it's not exactly the job of your dreams but in the same field, you will have a starting point.

A starting point

Your principal CV is what you create so that it sells your skills and traits in a very positive light and *will be the foundation from which all future CVs are born*.

You won't just have one 'catch-all' CV. If you do, and you're not getting interviews, then the reason is that you're not selling yourself directly to the job you're applying for.

One CV does not fit all jobs.
The principal CV will be the foundation from which all future CVs are born.

I don't want you to compile a CV that reads monotonously, that has no energy, or has no life experience. You probably won't be happy with the end product.

You will complete your CV more quickly and more professionally if you know your preferred job and industry, even if you're not very sure right this moment. Choose. Choose an area that is really appealing to you.

All employers are going to want to know some basic facts and see some qualities when they're reading your CV. For example,

- maturity;
- emotional intelligence;
- good communication – written and spoken;
- responsibility;
- integrity;
- problem solving skills;
- creativity;
- determination;
- compassion.

If you're about to leave school, work part time at college, during the summer, or want to secure some extra income or work experience, then you will need to show to a potential recruiter the relevant transferable experiences and learning in your life. Your career history will just be beginning, so you need to show you have qualities and skills gained from your life experience and employers can recognise these.

Employers are not daft. They can see how old you are. It's your job to convince them that your strengths and experience can be easily transferred to any situation or setting.

There is no denying that you may need some further training and induction, but then again, all new members of staff have to go through this process.

Transferable means *moveable, transportable, relocated, shifted, reassigned*. So when we talk of transferable skills, it means being able to move what you have into another situation or setting.

- Relocate them.
- Reassign them.
- Move them.

They aren't special skills – they're the skills you already have – the skills that everyone wants to have. The knack here is to show the employer that 'they're easily transferred'.

Recap
This is all about how you *transfer the skills and abilities* you have and express them in a CV so that an employer will snap you up.

It's true, employers do need experience in their workforce. Some won't budge on this; however, others are more open to consider people who show qualities that are flexible, passionate, innovative, determined, keen to learn and very committed to learning. It does depend on what the job is and what you hope to do.

When you send in a CV for a job, you will also write a good letter that is called 'a covering letter'. Here you will write about your strengths, values and abilities as well as relevant life experience. We'll cover that later in Part Two.

So, let's imagine.

You want to apply for a job with Apple. You have looked through the jobs that they advertise. You have chosen the one you think is most 'you'. You may not have all the skills they're seeking at this time, but the ad gives you a starting point.

The information that they have provided is a simplified *job description*, a brief overview of what they are expecting you to have and what they're seeking in a candidate.
Job descriptions can be brief, and sometimes they can go on for three or four pages. Depending on the age you are, the descriptions can vary between these goal posts.

Back to Apple.

You have read the job recruitment information about the type of person they're seeking. What would be your next step?

You create a CV from a template you've downloaded. You list, chronologically what you've done, when you've done it and what you're hoping to do, throw in a few personal interests and some brief work experience, a couple of references and upload it to their website.

Do you think you'll be invited to an interview?

- Maybe.
- Hoping.
- Not sure.

You may think that Apple would be an attractive place to work and you therefore will have to sell *your* skills to them based on the skills criteria they have outlined in the job specification.

'The skills criteria in the job specification?', I can hear you ask. 'Don't they just want to see who I am and what I have done?'

'Well, yes, they do, of course', I reply, 'but there's so much more they want to know and they have already given you a guide.'

Return to their website and if you haven't downloaded or viewed their job description and criteria of what they see as vital, then you won't be building a picture of *how to sell yourself to them.*

So first things first, this step is about gathering the material you will work with to develop, prove, draft, build and polish.

Activity 1.1: Go get it

Is there a job you want that is currently being advertised? A part-time casual job, voluntary work opportunity, or perhaps shadowing someone for work experience? Go get it. Go and print off the job advert and/or any job description, be it a small paragraph, a couple more, half a page, full page or two pages. Print it out and also save it to a folder on your desktop, if it's an online version.

What kind of job/work are you looking for? Be specific. The more clarity you have here, the easier your search will be.

_____

_____

_____

Write down the reason you want to create your first ever CV. How do you want this first CV to be used?

_____

_____

_____

What type of work is it? Part time/full time, how many hours? Is it voluntary, or a shadowing opportunity, perhaps a short-term research project?

_____

_____

_____

There may not be an abundance of information for you to read as often, if the job is informal, there isn't a large quantity of information. It's a few lines in a newspaper that says what they require and whom to contact. That's about it. That's OK. If this is the type of job you're after, then you just need to dig around a little more and ask for more information. That's why you need to be clear about why you're creating your first ever CV.

For now, we're beginning to build our principal CV and gather the information. You're not rushing to pull together a CV for a job.

If you find something that appeals and there's limited information, you could phone and ask them to send you some more details about the job via email or by post. However, you may find they don't have much and might even ask you about yourself on the phone while you're not prepared.

What I would suggest is to look further around this particular area and see whether there is something similar being offered at another company, with more information.

As I mentioned earlier, what you're looking for is a job description. This sometimes may be brief, but it ultimately 'describes the job' in more detail. You then need to look for an employee specification (sometimes called 'person specification'), which lists the employee requirements, usually separated into *essential* and *desirable*. All jobs should have something along these lines though it might be called different things by various recruiters.

You'll notice that recruiters sometimes list 'skills and attributes' that they require with an 'essential' column. Yes you guessed it, that means those skills are 'essential'. The 'desirable' column is normally something you don't necessarily need for the job, but it is really incredibly helpful and will support your job application.

Why am I telling you this?

Well, in this very competitive job market, you do need to stand out from everyone else who may be applying. It is not enough to just list skills and strengths, with no focus. By looking at the skills recruiters are seeking, in this gathering phase, you are beginning to form a foundation.

One CV does not fit all jobs.

The principal CV will be the foundation where all future CVs are born.

In order to create the principal CV, you have to gather together the skills employers are looking for and show how you are compatible with them.

Go and collect three jobs (jobs, work experience or voluntary) that are being advertised now or those that you intend to apply for. Print off the information. If it's all too long-winded, cut and paste the relevant information and keep all of it together in a folder. If this is online gathering, then create a specific folder for this information on your desktop. Paste any relevant facts into a brand new Word document and print it.

In **Step 2 – Develop It** our aim is to notice any similarities between the skills and attributes they require and the skills and attributes you possess. In a coaching session, these are some of the first things I would do with a client.

Take advantage

Take every opportunity there is to gain actual experience, whether that is in a current part-time job, a community centre, or an online forum, group or website. Attend extra courses or workshops, look at relevant web pages that relate to what you hope to do, approach voluntary organisations.

Once you have built your principal CV, you will have a document that displays your strengths, skills, attributes and experiences. You will be demonstrating self-motivation, drive and energy to succeed, and will be able to show that you have applied yourself to whatever weekend jobs or short snapshots of work/experience you have done. Working through this workbook will help you reveal insights about yourself and your values that would be attractive to a potential employer.

Activity 1.2: Go with the flow

For this next activity you're going to start collecting information about yourself. I want you to think of three people who know you very well and two people who don't. Going with the flow is similar to word association but with more focus on you and your skills, abilities and strengths.

Choose wisely. Don't just think of mum, grandma, friend. Think of the people who see you in action. These can be academic teachers, PE teachers, music tutors and sports coaches. Think a little outside the box. Who has seen you involved in a project? You may of course want to ask your family but I would keep a limit on a representation from them. Perhaps you have a careers advisor at school. The two people who don't know you very well could be someone who only sees you now and again. They're the kind of people who will have built up a picture of who you are and the kind of strengths that you project out to the world.

Here's what you're going to do.

Take each of your choices, one at a time. Give them a piece of A4 paper; on it you will have drawn five circles, about 2–3" wide. (No pressure on shape here, if you want to draw squares or triangles, diamonds, stars or hearts, that's absolutely fine!) Like this:

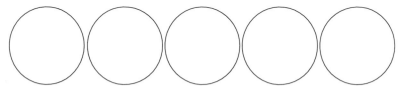

Inside each of the circles you're going to ask them to write positive things that they recognise in you: These can include:

- characteristics they notice;
- skills they admire;
- strengths that are evident;
- things that you're passionate about.

Here's an example for Jason as told by his music teacher:

Always on time *punctual*	Determined to better himself *ambitious*	Committed to practice *disciplined*	Public performer *confident*	Good humoured *funny*

This flow is Belinda's as told by her sports coach:

First to volunteer *enthusiastic*	Fundraises for charity *produces gigs and events*	Trains for competitive sport *dedicated*	Creates mini films *tech know-how*	Great at taking photos *creative*

When you sit with someone, hopefully you will find that they begin to 'flow associate', without much prompting from you. It tends to happen naturally. Often we don't ask people outright what they think, and when we do, we can be surprised by what we hear. Let this process evolve and see what happens. Don't forget to smile and say 'Thanks' rather than play down any of the compliments you receive, and you will receive them. Believe me.

Why not have a go at doing this with people that you feel confident with, first? It does take an ounce of courage to approach someone and ask them for five positive things about you. However, it is the first step of getting out there, assessing your skill set and recognising that you are doing something about building your first ever CV.

The point of doing this exercise before anything else is that you have to identify and recognise your own positive traits, skills, abilities and strengths. In the early flushes of writing your CV with someone, I always ask them to tell me five positive things about themselves and they often freeze up.

Doing this flow activity will start the ball rolling by involving others, giving you the confidence to gather the initial material and begin to build your skill set. So have fun with this. It will be interesting (and fabulous) to see what comes back from doing it.

> **Tip**
> It is best to give everyone a blank piece of A4 paper with the five flow circles already drawn. Avoid drawing all the flow circles on the same piece of paper as you don't want one person to be influenced by seeing what previous people have written.

By the end of this you will have approximately 25 completed flow circles. Of course, they don't all have to be filled and you may find there's an overlap with what they're saying. For example, there may be quite a few circles with 'confident', 'team player', or 'leader' in there. That's OK. At the time you notice they're saying the same thing about you, which could be a good thing. Maybe they are picking up on a strength of yours that you need to shout about. A strength, perhaps, that you didn't realise you had. Whatever they're writing, if you find the words are too similar, you can always ask them for an alternative.

There is also nothing stopping you asking more than five people. You can do this exercise ad infinitum. It's a great way of beginning a creative process where you gather together material that you can use later on in your CV.

Reciprocate the flows

It is a lovely thing to do – reciprocating the flow. This will work if you're doing this with family, friends, teachers etc. Why not do the same thing for them? It certainly will boost their confidence and at the same time will allow you to 'give something back'.

I remember when I was teaching a class at a sixth form college. We had come to the end of the module and wanted to finish the session with something positive. So I asked everyone to write his or her name on the top of a blank piece of paper. We then turned the page over and passed the page to the person seated to our right. This person then had to write something positive about the person sitting on their left, who had handed them the paper. They then folded down what they had written and passed it to the next person. It continued in this way where everyone was writing a positive thought, memory or snapshot of their classmate who sat on their left. This activity is just like the game 'consequences'. Do you remember this?

The pieces of paper worked their way around the entire class of 25 until they arrived back at the beginning. We had all received our own piece of paper back full of lovely positive comments that our classmates had written. Even I got one. As a teacher, working through a module with a group of students, you never quite know what they thought of your teaching and reading over the comments just made me realise why I was doing what I was doing, at that time. Everyone took turns to read out the comments. Some were funny, quaint, twee and downright positive. There were no nasty comments, just lovely, observant, comments and memories from the entire module.

This is the same kind of thing you will be doing with 'Going with the flow'. It can be difficult to promote yourself and say, 'I'm good at this, this and this'. We're so very eager to remember the negative traits. However, when you involve other people, whom you trust or admire, you begin to see how you 'project yourself' out into the world and how other people see you.

It is always a good place to begin.

Here write down all the words that you have gathered from the flow circles.

An extra element to this activity would be to take a look at the selection of words listed in the following columns and circle the ones that you think describe your skills, traits and abilities. Are there similarities with what your five chosen people have in their flow circles? Are there words that describe you but have been missed out? All of these words are extremely helpful in fine-tuning your profile but will also be useful at an interview.

adaptable	energetic	reliable
ambitious	imaginative	resourceful
assertive	independent	self-reliant
broad-minded	organised	cooperative
perceptive	self starter	creative
positive	tactful	imaginative
dependable	practical	talented
dedicated	problem solver	trustworthy
diplomatic	productive	team player
disciplined	punctual	efficient
realistic		

Activity 1.3: Start your timeline

Let's begin to assemble all the bits of regular information that are needed in a CV, things that will inform a potential recruiter. You can come back to this activity when you have the information and include it along the way.

At this early stage, we are not focusing on what your CV will look like. This is not the finished article; we're just gathering. For now, fill in the spaces with the information. If you would rather start this in a Word document and begin to type it up, then that's fine. Bear in mind though that there is no pressure to do this at this very early stage. I just want you to gather together the important information that will be needed. Remember to start with the most recent dates at all times.

1. **Name**: first and last names – you don't need middles unless you use them and want them there.

2. Contact details: address (include full postcode), phone number (landline and mobile), email address. If you have a cute and fancy email address then it's best to create a new one, which is in your name. Make sure all telephone numbers are correct.

Address:	**Telephone:**
	Mobile:
	Email:

3. Education: starting with the most recent, list the primary and secondary schools you attended; include postcodes and years you were there. If you have any other education (i.e. college or university) include this too. Remember to start with the most recent first.

From	To	School/college (including address)
Sep 93	Jul 00	St Josephine's, The Crescent, Kidderminster KR1 8TG

4. Qualifications: list here any examinations you have taken or are taking. Give the month and year plus the grade (if taken). Start with the most recent.

A Level:

Sep 10	Jul 12	History	(Grade: awaiting/pending)
		French	(Grade: awaiting/pending)
		English	(Grade: awaiting/pending)

GCSE:

Sep 08	Jul 10	Mathematics	Grade C
		English Language	Grade C
		English Literature	Grade B
		Science	Grade C

5. Work experience: make a note of any work experience you have. State the year and month, then a brief sentence (fitted on the same line) of your specific role.

Year	To	
2008	Jul–Sep	Receptionist at Leisure Centre, Fit Ness, Kidderminster

6. Voluntary work experience: again, as above. Note any voluntary experience you have done. State the year and the month, then a brief sentence (fitted on the same line of what you did and your specific role.)

Year		
2008	Weekly	Entertaining residents at residential home
2009	August	Organised charity event at community centre

The next activity encourages you to revisit the printouts you have gathered from jobs that interested you. As I mentioned earlier, these may be current jobs you're aiming to apply for, or they may be jobs where deadlines have passed but you're interested in that particular field.

It's important to reiterate why I am asking you to spend time looking at adverts, job descriptions and employee specifications. It may be crossing your mind that you aren't getting on with the task of creating the CV. Although it is not normally talked about when you are compiling your first ever CV, doing it this way is absolutely crucial because you are beginning to build a picture of what employers are seeking. Therefore I believe that it does form part of building the principal CV. It is the initial building block. The foundation.

What you're doing by gathering information is to create a CV that will inform someone who has never met you. The CV will tell them:

- where you've been;
- what you've been doing;
- what you're good at;
- where you've proved it;
- what you're passionate about;
- a bit about you and your personality.

When we sit down to write an assignment, a project, even an email, we know who's going to be reading it, right? We know what we have to do because we have a to-do list, or a set of criteria, or even an informal plan in our heads of what we need to say.

The reason we get caught up in the anxiety of creating a CV for the first time is that we don't know who is going to be reading it, we don't know what criteria we're trying to match up against, but more so, we don't know how to sell ourselves in a creative way: a way that makes us stand out.

I believe it is so much easier to have a guideline, something to work with, than a blank piece of paper.

Activity 1.4: Pruning – printed material

Earlier on I asked you to print out any jobs that you would like to apply for, either now or in the future. It doesn't matter if the deadline has passed, as long as you have a selection of the different types of jobs that are appealing to you. If you're looking at applying for voluntary work then collect any printed material about 'becoming a volunteer' and the skills or abilities needed for the role. If you are intending to apply for work experience, then dig around on the website of the companies you will be writing to and print off the job description that talks about the job roles you find interesting. Find something. Don't leave it – find some form of description and skill criteria for the job role you want.

In creating your principal CV, in the very first instance, you will find it easier if you base your CV on a particular role. It becomes more straightforward if you do it this way.

> **Tip**
> **If you are having difficulty finding descriptions or skills criteria for the job, unearth *a similar* job.**
> **There will be something out there that is related to it.**

- If it is an office clerk – find an alternative from another company.
- If it is a project worker – dig out the skills for this position.
- If it is a receptionist – locate a substitute.
- If it is a leisure assistant – uncover a description of the role.
- If it is a telephone call handler – discover another company.
- If it is a fashion retail assistant – get one from another company.
- If it is a dog walker – search for something that you can print off.
- If it is a gardener – dig up details from a landscaping company.
- If it is a charity fundraising – excavate a company that has this available.
- If it is an event worker – hunt for something that will give the skills needed.
- If it is a beauty therapist – ask for the job description.
- If it is a nursery assistant – track down an overview of the role.

Do you get my drift?

There is always something to discover, either at your local library or from your careers office at school/college. Failing these, go online or, if you're feeling more confident, ask to speak to a manager at a shop, business, charity, organisation or centre who could help. Be brave – you're doing research. Don't write them a letter or send them an email. Go and visit them.

Ask them:

'Do you have an outline or job description of this particular job? I am researching the essential and desirable criteria. Would it be possible to have a copy? Thank you so much.'

If they don't have anything, ask them if they could just very briefly list what skills, strengths, abilities, attributes, they would want to see as *essential* and are there any that are *desirable*? If they haven't got the time, then give them your email address and ask them to email you a brief list.

This whole activity shows that you

a)   have initiative;
b)   are approachable;
c)   can confidently ask for this research (irrespective of your age);
d)   communicate well.

If you were brave and ventured out and asked employers – hats off to you!

- Did you get any further information from them?
- Did they give you any insight about the kind of person they seek?
- What essential skills do they want?

Note down here any skills or strengths that they're seeking.

Activity 1.5: Pruning – online world

Gather together under one bookmark all the information you have found about particular organisations that are appealing to you so that it is easier to reference. When you have a little time, sit down and review some of these websites, and note down any strengths, skills or attributes that they keep repeating. Are the same things coming up all the time? What stands out for you in the online material?

Note down here the common strengths, skills and attributes you have noticed.

Develop It

This step is all about taking the information you have collected and starting to develop it. By now, you have found some job adverts, both online and locally. You are beginning to look at job descriptions and maybe read employee/person specifications; also, the language that they're using is becoming clearer. As mentioned earlier, sometimes with smaller jobs you may find that they just list *criteria*, so look out for this word too.

If you don't have an idea yet of the job that you want to apply for, I would say:

> **Just choose. Dream. Go on.**
> **Find three job adverts and criteria that really appeal to you.**

If you want to work for a DIY store, then hunt around their job page and print off/download any job descriptions.

Remember, you'll probably find jobs tucked at the bottom of a website, and it may say 'Career opportunities' 'Work with Us' 'Employment' or 'Careers'. What you're looking for is a 'description of the job'.

Let's look at a work experience placement that I found at BBC Radio Manchester, targeted at young people. It didn't take me long to find it. I visited www.bbc.co.uk and found their careers page. It was jam-packed. OK, it's competitive, but we're using *this detailing as an exercise only* to compile your principal CV, so don't feel pressured about it. Bear in mind here that we're looking at the *criteria* that they are seeking:

Drama Radio – Manchester   *Placement Length*: 1–3 Weeks

About the Department: This placement is to work in Radio Drama in Manchester, which produces about 50 hours of single plays and series for Radio 3, 4 and 7.

About the Placement: Please note that after shortlisting, we interview candidates and, if successful through both stages, you will be offered a placement. We discuss dates that work for the department and successful candidate and place after these discussions have taken place.

In the main instance placements are with the Production Co-ordinators which means that you will experience a vast range of tasks such as working in the Drama studio alongside the team, assisting with production paperwork and research or working with the development side of each area looking at scripts. If you are looking at technical/sound aspects, then we will try to match you with our technical experts. Work experience to us is a partnership and we try to tailor placements to meet the wishes of the individual with the day-to-day needs of the department. Placing you with the most appropriate mentor so that the placement is a rewarding experience.

Most placements will involve candidates in immediate contact with contributors, and it helps if those joining us on these schemes have some knowledge of the arts world.

Criteria: We're looking for applicants with a demonstrable interest in theatre and literature, who are keen Radio Drama listeners and have a grasp of some of our output already. The question on the form asking for a critique **must** be completed and relevant. It helps you to get greater fulfillment from our placements if you come with some experience as a consumer of what we do.

You should have good interpersonal skills, be creative and have excellent communication skills and IT skills. You need to be highly motivated, work well in a team, have good customer skills and be adaptable.

Applicants are advised to apply as soon as possible as we often place up to six months ahead.

Timetable for applications: placements available all year round.

Source: Job advert taken from www.bbc.co.uk

Let's break this down – just by reading and picking out what is already there.

Specific knowledge

- Interest in theatre and literature.
- Keen Radio 3, 4, 7 drama listener.
- Grasp and understanding of the output.

Skills and strengths

- Good interpersonal skills.
- Be creative.
- Excellent communication skills.
- Excellent IT skills.
- Highly motivated.
- Work well in a team.
- Good customer skills.
- Be adaptable.

Desirable/not essential

- Technical/sound experience.

Here you can see from that brief advert that the skills and strengths that they're looking for are right in front of us. I have created a mini criteria sheet, which shows what they want from an applicant. If you include and show aspects of evidence within your CV then you will be on to something. Of course, as they state in their advert, they also require a specific critique of a radio drama, which is a separate assessment procedure. For these purposes, we will just be using the criteria outline.

You can do this with any job that you find, even if there isn't a great deal of information available.

About person specifications

You may already be familiar with the term 'specification', particularly if you're studying for A levels, Access courses, BTEC Diplomas or HND. You will often have a 'criteria sheet' with the module you're studying and this gives a brief description about the module, the overall aims and objectives and actual criteria that you have to achieve.

For a particular essay, you may need to include specific criteria points, that are listed. That is the way an assessor will be marking your written work, by comparing what you have written to what they require.

> ### That's important to note:
> They will be comparing what *you* have written to what *they* require in order to pass.

You develop your essay response based on what they specify.

With a person specification, also known as an employee specification, the *employer* has written the required criteria and will be comparing what you have written to what they require, in order to pass.

They will write down a list of the skills, attributes, characteristics they require from the candidate and job and you have to prove to them how you meet the criteria in order to be invited to interview.

Let's bring this to life

Before I introduce you to **Activity 2.1: Craft a target job profile**, I'm going to include two different examples of a person specification that you will often find when you see a job advertised. If it is a more informal job, it may not be listed in this format. You may have seen an advert on a postcard in the post office window! It may be a bullet point list or a paragraph of information where you have to dig out the detail. If it's a voluntary job, you may not find anything apart from a generic job overview.

That's where Step One gives you support to gather this information. It will be worth while that you did.

As you progress through your career, you will become more familiar with person specifications and you will notice how they are used to complete application forms, develop CVs further and ultimately prove yourself to the recruiter.

Do you know why the person specifications exist? They are there for two reasons:

1. For the employer to specify what they want in an employee.
2. For you to assess if you meet the criteria for that particular job.

Many people read them and think:

- Good interpersonal skills   *Yes, I have that – tick that one*
- Be creative   *Ooh yes*
- Excellent communication skills *Definitely*
- Excellent IT skills   *Yes, got that*
- Highly motivated   *All the time*
- Work well in a team   *Oh yes – tick that as well*
- Good customer skills   *Clearly*
- Be adaptable   *Yes, got that too*

Then when they come to produce a CV for that job, they dilly-dally around these criteria and don't refer to them in the same way. They don't show and prove how they have achieved these criteria.

Again, person specifications *inform you* of the criteria that the employer wants from an applicant. The main aim is that *you* provide *them* with the evidence of how you meet each criterion and this will be used to shortlist you for interview.

> **If you provide examples, you will achieve a score.**

Therefore, before you begin to throw together a CV that has a list of your education, examinations, interests and work experiences, start to look at the appealing jobs and pick out the skills they're seeking. Work with this as your foundation.

Remember:

- One CV does not fit all jobs.
- The principal CV will be the foundation where all future CVs are born.

- In order to create the principal CV, you have to gather together the skills they seek and show how you are compatible with them.

Let's look at two specifications to identify this example: the two jobs I have chosen are for a receptionist and a web production manager. They are both different entry-level jobs, but they give us the opportunity to compare them, nonetheless.

The differences between essential and desirable criteria

I want you to really note the differences between the essential and desirable criteria as this will help you when you begin to craft your own **target job profile** in **Activity 2.1**.

Let's start to spot the skills they're seeking and see the similarities.

The differences between 'essential' and 'desirable' criteria

You must show how you meet the essential criteria by providing examples of times where you've done something similar.

Desirable is something they're not necessarily going to hold you to, but if there are numerous applications for the same job and all the applicants are providing evidence for the essential, then the recruiter will start to look at the desirable.

If you haven't any record of evidence for this, then you may be unsuccessful. So I would suggest that it is always preferable to add as much as you can.

Are you still wondering why we're doing this and not writing your CV? The difficulty with writing your CV is in the *detail*.

- Where do I start?
- What do I say?
- How can I show them I'm good?
- I don't have much work history, how do I prove my skills?

In spending time looking at person specifications and job descriptions, you will begin to build a picture of the type of job you're seeking and at the right level. You will be selecting skills and starting to provide evidence by the examples you have.

Nothing blooms from our brain when we have no research material. Everyone has to start from somewhere. If you're an artist and inspired by other artists' work – that's your base point. Perhaps if you're a retail business owner and you are starting a new company, you'll be referring to other companies – that's your base point. If you're a musician in a band, composing, you'll be referring to other music by similar artists – that's your base point.

> **There has always to be a base point. A point where you start.**

If you begin with just a blank page and pen, or a blank page on a screen, you'll feel overwhelmed by where to start.

I am helping you unpick this so that it doesn't have to be this way.

Let's look at a job description and person specification for a receptionist job at a county council (shown opposite).

You can see that this doesn't have a huge list of specific criteria. This job would be great for first time employment and will allow you to gain the skills in a working environment, giving you time and opportunity to develop further strengths.

If you were addressing these skills on your CV you would take each point separately to begin.

- **Education and training:**
  3 GCSEs or equivalent
    - You wouldn't have to mention this necessarily as this would be stated in the education section on your CV.
    - If you haven't taken your GCSEs yet, just state 'pending'.

Job title: Receptionist

Purpose of the job: To greet and assist visitors and answer incoming calls to reception.

Key tasks/principal accountabilities:
1. Receive/and deal with members of the public.

2. Assist customer care officers/or inform relevant officers.

3. Receive incoming calls and transfer to the appropriate extension.

4. Receive delivery of goods and direct to correct office.

5. Keep a comprehensive record of visitors to the department – i.e. visitor book.

6. Keep a weekly record of conference room bookings.

7. Ensure that the reception area is kept tidy at all times.

8. To provide administrative and clerical support to the planning services when reception duties have been fulfilled.

Person specification:

	Essential	Desirable
Education/training:	3 GCSEs or equivalent	
Experience:	Dealing with the public	Experience of working in an office Using Windows
Key qualities:	Possess good telephone manner	
Personal attributes:	Outgoing	Good organisational skills
	Welcoming personality Ability to work as part of a team	

- **Experience:**
  1. Experience of dealing with the public.
  Give them an example of when you have dealt with the public (if you think you haven't, you need to think closely about all you have done).

  2. Experience of working in an office.
  Can you tell them about a time when you have worked in an office environment (this can be paid or unpaid, for family, work experience, for free)?

  3. Using Windows PC
  Tell them when and how often you use Windows PC (if they specify Mac include it, but if you can work on both, then specify it) and give them an example of something you have done (Email, Internet, Word, Excel or PowerPoint).

- **Key qualities:**
  1. Possess a good telephone manner
  Give an example of where you have shown a good telephone manner. Be specific. Tell them the particular detail.

- **Personal attributes:**
  1. Outgoing welcoming personality
  Can you tell them about a time when you have shown this, perhaps at a school performance or a community event?

  2. Ability to work as part of a team
  Provide details of a time when you have worked in a team – in school, college, community or work.

  3. Desirable good organisational skills
  Provide evidence of a time when you have shown good organisational skills. **Give a specific example. Remember a time.**

Let's compare that and look now at the person specification for a web production manager.

Person specification for a web production manager

Qualification/education/training

Essential	Desirable
Design or web/related qualification	Awareness of dynamic languages such as PHP
Skilled in the use of Photoshop	
Good working knowledge of Microsoft Office	A management qualification
Sound knowledge of HTML	

Communication

Essential	Desirable
Internal	
External	
Phone	
Face-to-face	
Email	
In writing	

Skills

Essential	Desirable
Team player	Negotiation skills
Good listener	
Ability to talk to people of differing technical expertise	
Attention to detail	
Fantastic organisational skills	
Ability to work under pressure and to deadlines	
Ability to interpret data	

Knowledge

Essential	Desirable
Awareness of latest web technologies	Newspaper knowledge

If you were creating a CV to send to this employer, I would suggest you look at the essential column first. You will see four categories:

- qualifications/education/training;
- communication;
- skills;
- knowledge.

If you used these as headings you could then design your CV around these categories and take each criterion from Essential, give them an example and provide the evidence. You could omit the design/web-related qualification because they would see that when they viewed your CV qualifications.

Qualifications/professional training
Skilled in the use of Photoshop
Give an example of something you've created using Photoshop: a leaflet, brochure or photograph.

Good working knowledge of Microsoft Office
Give an example of where you have used Microsoft Office. Be specific with the detail.

Sound knowledge of HTML
Give an example of where you have used HTML.

If you want to include the desirables and you have the evidence to prove it – add this.

Awareness of dynamic languages such as PHP
Give an example of awareness of how you have used dynamic languages such as PHP.

A management qualification
This will be shown on your qualifications section on the CV.

You haven't had to make up any of this – the answers to their questions are all there.

The recruiter wants to know a time when you have:

- used Photoshop;
- used Office;
- used HTML.

And maybe, if they're lucky you will:

- show awareness of PHP.

All you have to do is think of the example. That's how they will review and assess your CV.

If you haven't done it, don't lie. If you have done it once and you were proud, then include it.

Hopefully you're getting a little taste of how you will develop the skills groups. You will design these based on what you have been discovering in Step One. As we progress, you will find that the formula will fall into place.

Take these small steps and familiarise yourself with the skill sets and criteria that you have.

You're beginning to develop and expand.

Activity 2.1: Craft a 'target job profile' (TJP)

For this you will need to take a large A3 piece of paper (A4 is fine, if that's all you have) and find some felt tips. It is so much more productive working with colour and has a huge impact on your brainwaves (check out the links at the back of the book to learn more about Mind Mapping).

Using the job descriptions and person specifications that I have included (including the work experience from the BBC) let's create our own TJP. A TJP is a collection of words that sum up the skills, strengths, attributes, characteristics and abilities that organisations are looking for in the candidate.

Work through the information and write down the following:

1. Words that *pop* out of the text at you.
2. Skills that are *repeated* by all of them.
3. Specific *skills* that are *relevant* to these jobs.

Let's see how it will look if I do it.

First I bring all of the criteria together on one page. You will be able to do this either online, in a Word document, or with the good old-fashioned method of pen and paper.

BBC Radio Drama – work experience
- interpersonal skills;
- creativity;
- communication skills;
- IT skills;
- motivation;
- team player;
- customer service skills;
- adaptability.

Receptionist vacancy
- dealing with the public – customer service;
- office skills;
- IT skills;
- good telephone manner – communication skills – speaking;
- polite, welcoming personality;
- team player.

Web production manager
- software and media skills, Photoshop, HTML;
- IT skills – Microsoft Office;
- communication – internal, external, phone, face to face, email, writing;
- team player;
- good listener;
- ability to talk to people of differing technical expertise;
- attention to detail;
- fantastic organisational skills;
- ability to work under pressure and to deadlines;
- ability to interpret data;
- positive outlook;
- a great balance of technical, commercial and people skills;
- awareness of the latest web technologies including video, podcasting.

I then spent time just looking through these three different lists and deleted any repetition – so I removed the word 'skills' and anything that was too wordy. I ended up with this:

- interpersonal;
- creativity;
- communication;
- IT skills – Microsoft;
- motivation;
- team player;
- customer service;
- adaptability;

- dealing with public;
- working in office;
- good telephone manner;
- polite, welcoming personality;

- software and media;
- Photoshop HTML;
- internal, external, phone, face to face, email, writing;
- good listener;
- ability to talk to people of differing technical expertise;
- attention to detail;
- fantastic organisational skills;
- ability to work under pressure and to deadlines;
- ability to interpret data;
- positive outlook;
- great balance of technical, commercial and people skills;
- awareness of latest web technologies including video, podcasting.

Now if I wanted to take it even shorter, I would really go through it again and be really strict. But for this purpose, it is fine. I will just remove the spacing in between and end up with this:

- interpersonal
- creativity
- communication
- IT~skills~Microsoft

- motivation;
- team~player;
- customer~service;
- adaptability;
- dealing~with~public;
- working~in~office;
- good~telephone~manner;
- polite~welcoming;
- software~and~media;
- Photoshop~HTML;
- internal~external~phone;
- face~to~face,~email,~writing;
- good~listener;
- ability~to~talk~to~people~of~differing~technical~expertise;
- attention~to~detail;
- fantastic~organisational;
- work~under~pressure~to~deadlines;
- interpret~data;
- positive~outlook;
- great~balance~of~technical,~commercial~people~skills;
- new~web~technologies.

It's important to use the ~ symbol (known as a tilde) for later work in Wordle (below).

That is now my target job profile (TJP) for the three jobs above. Usually, you would be looking at jobs that have similar skill sets and not vary as much as here. However, I wanted to show how this could be done.

If you can find volunteer jobs that you are going to apply for then you can work with the criteria that they have provided and build your TJP from this starting point.

Now that I have my TJP – I can keep it printed out, putting it to one side as I'm working with my principal CV. I can be aware of the skills, strengths, traits, characteristics, abilities that they're looking for and I can make sure that I include these in my principal CV.

However, because I'm a visual learner, I like things to look colourful. So, what I would do next is visit www.wordle.net. I'm sure you know all about Wordle. It's a great resource. A wonderful way for learning and remembering facts, data, or just merely presenting something in an innovative way.

In Wordle, I can paste my TJP into the available space and voilà.

> **If you want words to stay together, then you must place the 'tilde character' between words that go together. The tilde will then be converted to a space when drawing the words and they will be treated as a single word.**

You can spend quite a fair while with Wordle deciding on font, layout and colour. For this purpose I have used white on black as it is obviously being incorporated into this book. But if I were to print one out then I would have created a colour version.

In order to save your Wordle, you have to take a screen shot and save it as a PNG/JPEG, or you can print it straight away. You can also upload them to the public gallery but your Wordle creation will not be owned by you and anyone can use it.

Moving on to assessing your own skills and strengths you are now going to review your own skills categories. In order to feel confident you have to know what they are, so that if I stopped you in the street and said, 'I'm recruiting for a job, tell me what your top three strengths are', you'd be able to tell me. You'd be positive, convincing, and in no doubt that you know what you're talking about.

If I asked you to give me an example of when you showed a strength, you'd be even more joyful as you proudly tell me.

So by the time you have completed the next **Activity 2.2: Taking stock of strengths and skills**, you are going to feel more certain.

I can't stress this enough: it is vital to explore your skill sets and your strengths in order to translate these into your principal CV because you will be able to show how transferable you really are irrespective of your employment history.

Activity 2.2: Taking stock of strengths and skills

In this activity, you'll find 78 questions split into 13 groups. Read each statement either to yourself or out loud. Give yourself a score out of 10 for each one (1 = not so great, 10 = really fabulous). Be gentle with yourself, don't be too self-critical – assess this carefully.

A key may also be useful: Scores over 8

Scores over 6

Scores over 4

Scores below 3 🚫

I'm not going to make you add up the scores or put you into a specific box, or tell you that you must work harder. That is not what this exercise is about. The idea behind this is to give you an overview of where you see your skills lie and, ultimately, for you to choose the categories where you feel you have the most strengths.

By completing this activity you will begin to see that you have key strengths. I will show you how you can build on these strengths to give examples and evidence, so that when a potential recruiter begins to read your CV, it will stand out with your transferable experience.

If you feel that there are some weaknesses, don't worry about this. The only reason we're looking at this is to discover your strongest set.

This could be a good activity to do once on your own and then reflect upon it at a later stage with one (or all) of the people you chose for your flows (see Activity 1.2).

You will notice that I have underlined certain words in each of the statements, I will refer to this later but for now just begin. When you don't have a great deal of experience or work history, it's a great way for you to demonstrate that someone needs to take a chance on you.

1. Reading skills: Communication

1. I feel confident about reading.
2. I can read information from a wide variety of different sources.
3. I can read books relevant to my chosen subject, disregarding books that aren't necessary.
4. I can skim read, scan and read in-depth.
5. I can make useful notes when I'm reading and researching for a piece of work. I can also read them back.
6. When reading a piece of text, I can sum up the main points.

2. Writing skills: Communication

7. I can write my ideas in a confident way.
8. I can write reports, essays and letters.
9. I plan essays and assignments before the writing stage.
10. Before submitting a piece of work, I always check for spelling and grammatical errors.
11. My work is well presented.
12. When in lessons, presentations, and/or demonstrations, I can read back any notes I have made.

3. Speaking skills: Communication

13. I <u>feel confident explaining things</u> to other people.
14. I would be <u>able to give a presentation</u> to a group.
15. I can <u>explain visual aids</u> confidently in a presentation.
16. I <u>listen and ask appropriate questions</u> during discussions.
17. I can <u>ask questions of people I don't know</u>.
18. I can speak without any notes.

4. Teamwork

19. I have <u>worked as part of a team</u>.
20. I like to be an instrumental member in a team.
21. I like <u>to include others</u> who maybe are not contributing.
22. I am <u>happy to lead</u> if the opportunity arises.
23. I am <u>eager to report any difficulties</u> to the team.
24. I like to <u>keep to schedules</u> and monitor progress.

5. Solving problems

25. When I have <u>work to do, I split it up</u> into smaller tasks.
26. If I don't understand a problem, I seek help.
27. I <u>enjoy solving problems</u>.
28. When given a new task, I like to <u>produce various ideas</u>.
29. I prefer to think about a goal before deciding on what action to take.
30. I always <u>think about alternatives</u> to solving problems.

6. Personal management

31. I <u>organise my work well</u> in order to meet deadlines.
32. I <u>always check my progress</u> as I'm working.
33. When it comes to managing my time and getting things done, I know what I'm good at and not so good.
34. I know <u>where to go and find support</u> when I need it.
35. I <u>have a future vision</u> in my mind.
36. I like to <u>discuss my plans</u> with family or friends.

7. Working with numbers

37. When making <u>simple calculations</u>, I feel confident.
38. I <u>use a calculator, if need be</u>, in my studies/work/job.
39. I <u>am confident working with fractions, decimals and percentages</u>.
40. I am <u>able to construct graphs, charts</u>, and diagrams.
41. I <u>can interpret graphs and charts</u> if necessary.
42. I am <u>confident handling statistics</u> as part of my job or my coursework.

8. IT (information technology)

43. I can <u>use a word-processing package</u> to produce my work.
44. I can <u>use a spreadsheet</u> whenever necessary.
45. I can <u>use a database</u> package.
46. I am <u>confident in researching on the Internet</u>.
47. I <u>can produce a presentation</u> using software.
48. I feel <u>confident using audio-visual equipment</u>.

9. Creativity

49. I <u>visualise an ambition</u> for myself.
50. I <u>break down big tasks</u> into little chunks.
51. I <u>turn negatives into positives</u> and find ways through.
52. I see <u>different perspectives</u> and look at new ideas.
53. I <u>use my intuition</u> when completing tasks.
54. I <u>help others</u> to be creative.

10. Media

55. I <u>turn my visual ideas into media reality.</u>
56. I use <u>various forms</u> of media, e.g. blogs, websites.
57. I am confident <u>of using software</u> that can help my creativity.
58. I can teach myself new software packages, e.g. camera, HD video.
59. I can <u>fix equipment</u> when it goes wrong, calmly.
60. I can <u>produce resources</u> from my media.

11. Working with people

61. I understand other people and <u>can build positive relation-ships</u>.
62. I <u>support others</u> and encourage their views.
63. I <u>inspire/nurture people</u> in my community.
64. I share my views with others confidently.
65. I <u>handle conflict</u> in a mature way.
66. I <u>work equally with others</u> to arrange group tasks.

12. Being an entrepreneur

67. I <u>build positive relationships</u> with people who are not in my peer group.
68. I <u>see every opportunity</u> and develop new projects.
69. I <u>use my initiative</u> and <u>sometimes take risks</u> with new things.
70. I <u>handle pressure well</u> and cope with being let down.
71. I <u>identify what people want</u> and turn it into action.
72. I have ideas about how other people can do things.

13. Administration

73. I have a system enabling me to <u>manage my personal money</u> well.
74. I <u>run a small budget</u> for a team/group.
75. I <u>have a good filing system</u> for my online documentation.
76. I have a good filing system for my personal documentation.
77. I know where to go to find paperwork that I need.
78. I keep all my certificates in one place.

From this activity, jot down:

Which categories scored the most?

Which ones had the most hearts?

Did you have many smiley faces? ☺ Which ones?

On which individual criteria did you score yourself the highest?
Write them again here.

Did any scores surprise you? What was the surprise?

Activity 2.3: Five chief skill categories

You now have to choose your top five categories (from 13) –
those that had the most hearts and smileys and sum you up
beautifully.

1. [   ]

2. [   ]

3. [   ]

4. [   ]

5. [   ]

If you are having difficulty choosing, then go back and do the
activity again, only this time think about where you feel you
really shine. Give yourself a mark out of 10, assess yourself
confidently and if you would like, as I mentioned before, you
could do this activity with a parent, teacher, mentor, family
member, group leader, sports coach, part-time manager, or
close friend.

Prove It

By this point, you will be noticing a pattern emerging of your strengths and skills. Are you seeing some areas that are strong and some that aren't? We are building towards thinking about evidence and soon you're going to be able to *prove* some of these skills/strengths.

What do I mean by proving some of these skills/strengths?

It will become clear as we skip along, but for now, what does the word 'prove' mean? It means 'establishing or helping to establish a fact or the truth of a statement'.

You may also be familiar with these other words that can mean proof:

- verification;
- confirmation;
- corroboration;
- testimony;
- evidence.

In Step Two I asked you to decide on your five chief skills – keep these in mind as you begin the next activity. I'm going to give you some categories and I want you to think of proof relating to them. They may not be your chief skills but will provide you with an example when thinking about providing evidence.

Activity 3.1: Reveal more
Let's now reveal a little bit more. I'd like you to answer the

following questions. Imagine that I am asking you these questions as if we are sitting opposite one another. It isn't a test, there is no one assessing you. If you can, write bullet point sentences. Don't write long-winded paragraphs.

This is what I call 'initial blooming': the first phase of putting short snappy sentences together – think of the evidence. Then, just let your thoughts instinctively emerge and don't force them. If you're struggling because you can't think of what to write, take a little time out and revisit the categories earlier and read over your notes so far from the activities.

To help you with this activity I am going to introduce to you T-REX. This is an acronym for

Task

Response

Ending

e**X**act

This is something I devised to help with writing a first-time CV at this level – the main aim I am hoping for is that you are *exact with your examples*. It can help with writing application forms and expression statements for jobs and it can be really useful when you're at an interview. It helps to cut out the waffle.

Yes, you heard me. I said 'waffle'. I have been there myself – in the past, I used to waffle like crazy in application forms and whenever I needed to write an expression statement. Through experience and some nifty tools (ones that I'm passing on to you), I developed a much more friendly way of writing my evidence.

T-REX is what I want you think about when you do this next activity.

- Think of the Task – jot down what it was.

- Think of the Response – what were you doing? What was your role? Keep it brief.

- Think of the Ending – what happened? How did it play out in the end?

■ Think of being eXact– be specific with your example – give the detail.

Communication – speaking

1. Give me an *exact* example of when you have spoken well. This could be with a team of younger pupils in the school. It could be when you overcame a difficult situation and spoke out. It could be a debate, a meeting or an assembly. It could be in school, in a team, at a youth group, theatre, etc.

Think of the Task
Think of the Response
Think of the Ending
Be eXact

Can you think of another time?

IT (information technology)

2. Tell me an exact situation where you used your IT skills. Don't just tell me when you completed a project, write the exact details. Did you design an Excel spreadsheet for coursework? What was it? Have you developed an Access database for a group mail out? Have you created flyers, posters or brochures in Word?

Think of the Task
Think of the Response
Think of the Ending
Be eXact

Can you think of another time?

Media

3. Provide me with the *exact* details of any media projects you have created and whether these were for personal, communal, work, or school related. Have you designed your own blog or website? Do you manage a forum? Have you created mini films? Are you adept at using Photoshop?

    Think of the Task
    Think of the Response
    Think of the Ending
    Be eXact

Can you think of another time?

Personal management

4. Think of a time when you have organised yourself really well. It could be coursework, managing different assignments, helping a community project, training for an important sports occasion as well as working.

    Think of the Task
    Think of the Response
    Think of the Ending
    Be eXact

Can you think of another time?

As you may not have extensive work experience, it is crucial to think 'outside the box' and dig deep relating to anything where you put your energy.

If you take time to answer these questions, you will be making a start on building your own CV evidence that will be incorporated into your principal CV. There's no pressure to answer these in one sitting. The whole purpose of this book is to be able to pick it up, answer a few questions, have a break and return when you're feeling receptive to them. Give them a go. I also find that when you continue with more activities throughout the book, you will find more things to write and add things as they occur to you.

It may also be worth bearing in mind that questions like these could be asked during an interview. If you're invited to attend, you'll be able to revisit your answers for inspiration and reminders. There is more information about interviews in Part Three.

Why are we doing this?

When a potential recruiter reads your covering letter and CV, they will be scanning for evidence and examples of what you have done. They will also be looking for signs of your enthusiasm and eagerness to work with them. They want to confirm that you are a mature individual and potential employee/volunteer, therefore you need a good quality summary of your own qualities and strengths.

They'll be thinking:

- Can you work under pressure?
- Will you be able to cope?
- Can you deal with the general day to day tasks?
- Does your CV demonstrate that you're a hardworking, reliable and committed individual?
- Can you show them that you will be an ideal candidate?

You have to prove that you are an applicant whom they would like to interview. Ultimately, the purpose of your CV is to secure an interview. It is the first step in the process.

All employers will be asking themselves the above questions about a potential job applicant, whether that is for work experience, voluntary work, or paid employment. It doesn't matter if it's the corner shop, a big retail store, your local museum or a telephone call handler, they still want to know:

- Does this applicant have a good set of skills and strengths?

- Do they illustrate their skills and strengths with examples and explain where they have used them?

> **Remember – a potential employer spends approximately one minute reading your CV.**
> **It has to grab them in that first minute.**

All applicants need to provide evidence. Usually this will happen while filling in an application form and writing an expression statement. However, in creating your CV for the very first time, and with limited employment history to show, it is important to bring out the strengths and skills you do have by giving examples of when you have done something similar.

I don't want you to assume that because you haven't much work history, you are not going to get the job, voluntary opportunity or work experience. When you've completed your CV (having followed these seven steps), employers will be surprised and delighted to read it.

Employers and voluntary organisations will be looking for creativity, communication, initiative, drive, determination, great team-working skills, independence, planning and organisation. It's all about the evidence.

The next activity is similar to the previous one, but it focuses more on the skill categories. Before you warm up with your own skill categories I will give you a chance to immerse yourself in the next exercise. I will give you an example of each skill and strength so that you have an idea of what I'm asking you to do. You don't have to use these in your principal CV, but you may want to do just that. When creating your principal CV you can have as many skill categories as you like but when sending off a CV or uploading to a website, you should not exceed more than two pages and it should be more tailor-made to the job you're seeking. Consequently, you can draw on these examples.

Whenever you send your CV out for a new job, or experience, you will choose your five chief skills categories. However, you can add another category to help fit with the job description and person specification or take one away. This you will find from your target job profile (TJP). Always create a TJP!

And remember T-REX:

- Think of the Task – jot down what it was.
- Think of the Response – what were you doing? What was your role? Keep it brief.
- Think of the Ending – what happened? How did it play out in the end?
- Think of being eXact – be specific with your example – give the detail.

Activity 3.2: Skill surprise
Communication (speaking)

I created a presentation about my fundraising work in Africa and delivered it to over 150 parents at a school open evening.

Communication (listening)

I volunteered for a college project where I was a buddy to an elderly resident and I telephoned them once a week for a chat.

Organisation

I coordinated the sale of tickets for our amateur dramatic

production of 'Oliver' at our local community centre.

Working independently

For my business GCSE coursework, I carried out face-to-face questionnaires, which I then had to analyse and incorporate into a group presentation.

Dealing with deadlines

When completing my Access course I also had a part-time job. I developed ways of managing my time by keeping a schedule on my mobile phone, with prompts and alerts to remind me what I was doing and when.

Team work

As a member of my netball team, I make sure I work towards the group aim and we recently reached the top four in the national league.

Information technology

Having worked on a PC for five years, I now am confident with Microsoft packages and keeping an email database with Excel for the contacts for my brother's building firm.

Using initiative

Nearing completion of my coursework for psychology, my computer suddenly froze. I had lost my most recent work. I now make sure I save my writing on my USB drive every 10 minutes as well as sending an email to myself with my attached work. I always think things through and learn from experiences.

Specific talents

I always think of new ways to raise money for Macmillan Cancer Support. Last month I organised a cake sale through my school and raised £400 by selling muffins bought from a large wholesaler.

If you want to replace some of the skills I have chosen here with those from **Activity 2.2: Taking stock of strengths and skills**, please do so.

It is good that you're thinking this way, developing your skill set and fine-tuning it, based on the types of jobs you are seeking.

For example, if you're going to apply for more creative jobs, you may want a creative and media section. However, bear in mind that employers still need to see that you're communicative, organised, good at working in teams and able to manage your own workload.

Employers are always on the look-out for examples of the above categories.
This is why they're called employability skills.

By now you will be developing a clearer picture of your strengths and 'who you are' and providing particular examples. You can see the similarities between the skills that employers are seeking and the evidence that you are collecting.

I trust that you are beginning to see what you have to offer and how it matches with the target job profile that you have created earlier in Activity 2.1.

Your pitch is getting stronger.

Any time you have an idea or think of an experience that you have had or a skill that you can demonstrate, add it here. Don't worry right now about structure and wording. This will all materialise later. For now, record the thought and carry on with whatever else you're doing.

Step Four

Draft It

Creating your first draft CV

This is the place when all the gathering, developing and proving comes together.

By now, you will have:

- a clearer idea of the types of jobs that you're seeking;

- an idea what a job description and a person specification look like;

- followed the process as I created a target job profile;

- created your own target job profile based on the job adverts and person specifications you have found, collecting an array of interesting skills, strengths, abilities and attributes;

- identified your five chief skills after analysing your own strengths and skills;

- examples from your own life experience to demonstrate your skills;

- noticed the transferability between your skills and the skills being asked for.

As I mentioned above, employers and recruiters will spend a very small amount of time reading your CV – about a minute, not enough time for them to read all about you. This means you have to present your information in a way that doesn't discard you within that minute. This could mean working on things like:

- spelling and grammar;

- sentence construction;

- spacing and layout;

- font and size;

- paper quality – if you're printing it out;

- Microsoft Word compatibility – if you're uploading it.

(We will be looking at these later in Step 6 – Polish It.)

You may want to pursue roles in the creative industries, which doesn't mean that you pull out all the stops and load the CV with colour, photographs and your creative exploits. This really is best left until the interview where you can take along your portfolio and it will be welcomed with open arms.

Skills and achievements that are not work related can be a real eye opener for employers about the kind of person you are and your attributes. For example, organising and coordinating, managing people, entrepreneurship, determination, patience, planning, selling and marketing, purchasing and production, creating things, developing and building things and technical competence and expertise.

Activity 4.1: Draw up the CV structure

In Step 1, **Activity 1.3: 'Start your timeline'**, you were asked to begin to collect the important information that you may need and encouraged to fill in the boxes. This next step, 'Draft it' is where you start to take another step forward and create your principal CV in a Word document.

If you have already done this, then, well done you! If you haven't (and there was no pressure to do so), begin to do this now. As I have mentioned before, there are templates available online and in books, so if you would prefer to use one that you have already, that's fine. For the rest of you, here's my simple structure to start off this process of writing your CV.

Put your name here

32 CV Road   0151 123 4567
Russell Village   09821 123 456
Liverpool   myname@email.com
L1 7RN

Profile
[This is where you are going to put a few sentences that capture who you are, what your chief skills are and what strengths you have. We will be getting to this later.]

Education and qualifications
[List your education starting from the most recent accompanied by qualifications]

Month   Year   Place

Key skills and abilities
[For each of these examples – this is where you put your evidence and specific illustration. Don't worry if it is not on one line – just record the particular evidence that confirms you have this chief skill.]

Chief skill category 1
[Example]
[Example]
[Example]

Chief skill category 2
[Example]
[Example]
[Example]

Chief skill category 3
[Example]
[Example]
[Example]

Chief skill category 4
[Example]
[Example]
[Example]

Chief skill category 5
[Example]
[Example]
[Example]

Work history (if applicable)
[List any full-time or part-time jobs you have had, beginning with the most recent. Include dates you were there, the job title and the name of the employer, for example:]

| Jun 11 | Sep 11 | Retail assistant | TK Maxx Liverpool f/t |
| Sep 09 | May 11 | Usherette | Showcase Cinemas p/t |

Work experience
[Any work experience you have had while at school or college could be placed in this section and this may also include any voluntary work.

If you really don't have much work experience, don't lie or expand the truth. That's why we are creating a skills-based CV so that we can show the potential recruiter that you are still a candidate to consider. You may not have vast quantities of work history, but we all have to start somewhere. If you would prefer to delete this section, that's OK.

If you wish to keep it in, you could re-name it. Perhaps list 'course work and projects' that you have done at school or college. If you are training/learning at night school then it may be benefical to state what specific projects you're working on.

This would also be a place to mention any extra curricular activities that you are involved in. For example, anything to do with the local community centre, church/religious group, amateur dramatics, sports, anything that shows you are engaged.]

Hobbies and interests
[Recording your interests will give any potential employer an idea of what you're like and the type of person you are. This section is often a rich source of achievement. Many people often throw themselves into an activity or passion and this will highlight their energy, drive and motivation to potential employers.]

References
[Give two references.]

Name:
Position:
Available on request.

[You need to ask your referees if they will act as a reference for you before you start including their name. Don't include them if you haven't asked to do so. Use people who are current in your life, not someone from a year ago whom you don't contact, or who doesn't know what you're doing. You can also ask teachers or people in your community. You don't need to include their address details, just give details as shown above.]

So that's the long and short of it. You will notice that these sections feel familiar and that's because you will already have the information to hand from earlier in the book.

You don't have to choose five chief skill groups: if you find you only have three chief skills, that's fine. If you want to use more that's OK, *but do not exceed two pages of A4 when you send your CV to a potential recruiter.* It is just too long and they won't read it.

If you would like to create an extended principal CV and use all 13 skills categories with your examples of evidence, that's great. However, remember to choose your top five chief skills when you send/upload it, relate this to the target job profile you created for the job. Keep in mind the skills they require. This is what they will be looking at when they're reviewing your CV.

Select a format you like and stick with it.

Remember that when you have completed more work experiences, you will have expanded your knowledge base, with new examples to share, so don't forget to add them too. This will then make your CV stand out more.

> **What I want you to realise – is that just because you haven't had a long employment history doesn't mean that you can't demonstrate where you have done something similar.**

Activity 4.2: Outline your profile

Being asked to write a profile statement can sometimes be met with a sharp intake of breath. Where do I start? First, you have to put aside the shy part of you that doesn't like selling yourself. Your profile is the first section of writing that a potential recruiter will read about you – and often, if they're short of time, it is the main area for them to read. So it has to summarise you very well.

What I want you to do now is go and find all the flows you have for **Activity 1.2 Go with the flow** and write down here all the words that you have (avoid any repetition):

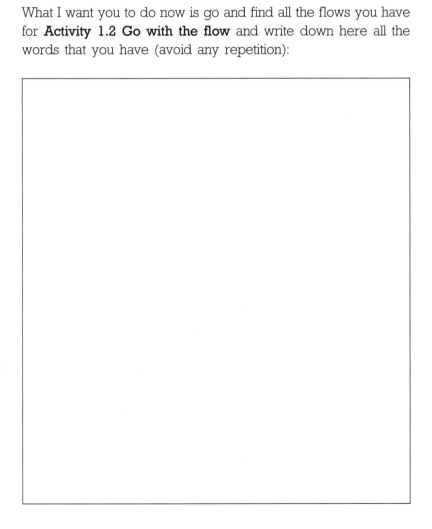

From these words you will have a selection that may 'sum you up'. You're going to start thinking about forming them into a sentence.

Revisit **Activity 2.2: Taking stock of strengths and skills** and notice the words that I have underlined. If you have scored yourself highly with these statements, then those underlined words could also be really helpful in describing you and your abilities.

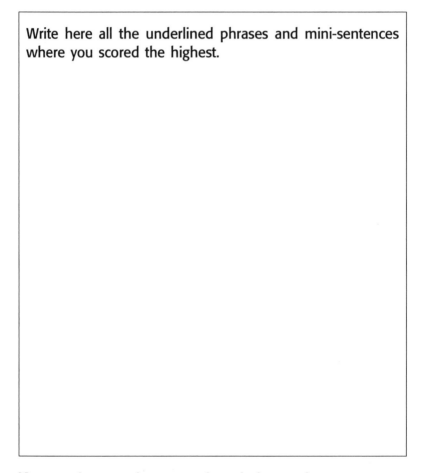

Write here all the underlined phrases and mini-sentences where you scored the highest.

Now you have to choose words and phrases that sum you up. Think of small sentences that describe you from all the information you have gathered. If you were to have 30 seconds to read out who you were, what you were good at and what your top five chief skills are, what would you say?

Let's look at the kind of thing I'm suggesting you create.

Example 1: Profile of 17-year-old Tom

Apple enthusiast and excellent communicator who loves to be the first to help and to share knowledge with others about Apple products. Proficient at fixing computer problems. Up to date with all products in their range. Good at building positive relationships and friendships in school and community. Appetite for meeting new people. Great listener and helper, with a patient manner. Creative artist with a love of writing poetry and digital photography using iPhoto, iMovie, iWork and Photoshop software. Extreme love of travel, raising money for worthy causes and working independently; using initiative at every twist and turn, taking every opportunity that arises.

Example 2: Profile of 18-year-old Jessica

Fully qualified beauty therapist professional, with enthusiasm and dedication. A real addition to your team. Extremely capable, working independently, with minimum supervision. Keen to share and learn new techniques and skills. Good interaction and interpersonal capabilities with customers and team members. Bubbly personality and good sense of humour. Always striving for the best outcome with clients, priding myself on my beauty skills. Great deal of experience working in different situations due to variety of summer jobs, gap year in another country and heavy involvement with communal events.

How to reduce the word count

Sometimes when we start writing our profiles we have too many words in the sentences and they're very long winded. It has to be punchy, to the point and explain your skills, strengths, passions, capabilities and character.

With long-winded sentences I always suggest removing all the 'itsy bitsy' words. I'll show you what I mean; here are Tom's profiles before and after.

Before – Example 1: Tom

I am an Apple enthusiast and have excellent communication skills. I really love to be the first to help and to share knowledge with others about all of the Apple products, as well as being very capable at fixing other computer problems. I am extremely knowledgeable and up to date with all their products in the range and extremely good at building positive relationships and friendships with people, not just in school, but also in my community as well. I have a real appetite for meeting new people. I am a great listener and productive helper with a very patient manner. I am also a creative artist with a love of writing poetry and using digital photography such as iPhoto, iMovie, iWork and Photoshop software. I have an extreme love of travel and raise money for worthy causes in the Third World. I can work independently and use my initiative at every twist and turn taking every opportunity that arises. (160 words)

(In making changes you can see how the 'itsy bitsy' words were removed.)

After – Example 1: Tom

Apple enthusiast and excellent communicator who loves to be the first to help and to share knowledge with others about Apple products and proficient at fixing computer problems. Up to date with all products in their range. Good at building positive relationships and friendships in school and community. Appetite for meeting new people. Great listener and helper with a patient manner. Creative artist with a love of writing poetry and digital photography using iPhoto, iMovie, iWork and Photoshop software. Extreme love of travel, raising money for worthy causes, working independently, using initiative at every twist and turn, taking every opportunity that arises. (100 words)

Before – Example 2: Jessica

A fully qualified beauty therapist working in an extremely professional way, with enthusiasm and dedication, who will be a great addition to your team. Very able to work both independently and with minimum supervision. Keen to share and learn new techniques and skills. Good interaction skills, with people and other team members, having a bubbly personality and a good sense of humour. Always striving for the best outcome with clients. Pride in my work is very important. Great deal of experience working in different situations due to variety of summer jobs, a gap year away in another country and much involvement within community events. (104 words)

After – Example 2: Jessica

Fully qualified beauty therapist professional, with enthusiasm and dedication – an asset to your team. Extremely capable, working independently, with minimum supervision. Keen to share and learn new techniques and skills. Good interaction and interpersonal capabilities with customers and team members. Bubbly personality and good sense of humour. Always striving for the best outcome with clients, priding myself on my beauty skills. Great deal of experience working in different situations due to variety of summer jobs, gap year in another country and heavy involvement with communal events. (86 words)

A profile can be short, punchy, snappy and to the point. You don't have to write a paragraph that reads like a piece of writing. I would encourage you to look at what you have gathered and then start to manipulate this information, so it gives an overview of *you* – in a nutshell.

Build It

How to build your principal CV

You may realise that by now you are building your CV, layer by layer. It's like any project where you build piece by piece, segment by segment, breaking in gently, preparing the foundations, nurturing the ground and slowly building something so that when it is complete, it will tell a fuller, more beautiful story about you. It is a little like a triangle leading up to the pinnacle. You're preparing the ground.

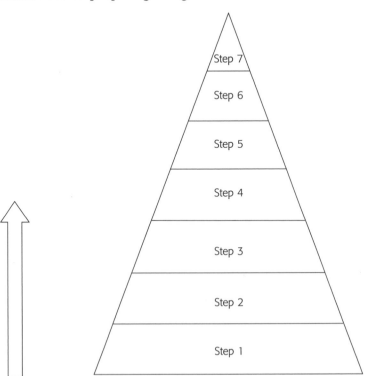

We are therefore going to continue to build another layer and tweak your chief skills.

Activity 5.1: Tweak your chief skills

Above in **3.1**, **3.2** and **4.1**, I asked you to think of examples for each of your five chief skills. I'd like you to bring them forward and write them in the following box.

```
Chief skill 1
*
*
*

Chief skill 2
*
*
*

Chief skill 3
*
*
*

Chief skill 4
*
*
*

Chief skill 5
*
*
*
```

Our ultimate aim for your CV is to fit all of these examples onto one line. This can be a little tricky, but again, it's about removing the 'itsy bitsy words' and lengthening margins as well as changing fonts. Due to the constraints within this book, the sentences may extend over one line, but that is because the margins are not adaptable. However, you will be able to do that with your own Word document. It is similar to what you did with your personal profile.

Let's look at how to do this, using the examples that I gave earlier.

Communication skills – Writing, reading, presenting (Chief skill 1)

* I created a presentation about my fundraising work in Africa and delivered it to over 150 parents at a school open evening.
* I volunteered for a college project where I was a buddy for an elderly resident and I telephoned them once a week for chat.

By removing the 'itsy bitsy' words this would read:

* Created presentation, delivering it to over 150 parents at open evening.
* Volunteered as listening ear buddy for elderly residents in the community.

Organisation skills (Chief skill 2)

* I coordinated the sale of tickets for our amateur dramatic production of 'Oliver' at our local community centre.

And, by removing 'itsy bitsy' words:

* Produced and coordinated sale of tickets for our community centre production of 'Oliver'.

Working independently (Chief skill 3)

* For my business GCSE coursework, I carried out face-to-face questionnaires, which I then had to analyse and incorporate into a group presentation.

And, by removing 'itsy bitsy' words:

* For GCSE business project, completed questionnaires, analysed data, presented to group.

Dealing with deadlines (Chief skill 4)

*   When completing my Access course I also had a part-time job. I developed ways of managing my time by keeping a schedule on my phone, with prompts and alerts to remind me of what I was doing and when.

When the small words are deleted, this becomes:

*   Developed good strategies for managing my times when completing my Access course.

Team work (Chief skill 5)

*   As a member of my netball team, I make sure I work towards the group aim and we recently reached the top four in the national league.

This can be cut down to:

*   Reached the top four in the National Netball League by working well as a team.

Information technology (Chief skill 6)

*   Having worked on a PC for five years, I now am confident working with Microsoft packages and keeping an email database with Excel for the contacts for my brother's building firm.

This now reads:

*   Confident working on all Microsoft packages; creating Excel database for brother's firm.

Using initiative (Chief skill 7)

*   Nearing completion of my coursework for psychology, my computer suddenly froze. I had lost my most recent work. Now I make sure I save my writing on my USB drive every 10 minutes as well as sending an email to myself with my attached work. I always think things through and learn from experiences.

After editing, this becomes:

*   Overcame potential loss of files when power failed on my computer by saving on USB.

Specific talents (Chief skill 8)

*   I think of new ways to raise money for Macmillan Cancer Support. Last month I organised a cake sale through my school and raised £400 by selling muffins bought from a large wholesaler.

We can cut this to:

*   Innovative fundraiser for Macmillan Cancer Support raising money selling cakes in school.

When you do this, your CV structure will begin to look like this:

Key skills and abilities

Communication skills – reading, writing, presenting

*   Created fundraising presentation, delivering it to over 150 parents at open evening.
*   Volunteered as listening ear buddy for elderly residents in the community.

Organisational skills

*   Produced and coordinated sale of tickets for our community centre production of 'Oliver'.
*
*

Researching skills and working independently

*   GCSE Business project, completed questionnaires, analysed data, presented to group.
*
*

Dealing with deadlines

* Developed good strategies for managing my time when completing my Access course.
*
*

Teamwork

* Reached the top four in the National Netball League by working well as a team.
*
*

Information technology

* Confident working on all Microsoft packages; creating Excel database for brother's firm.
*
*

Using initiative

* Overcame potential loss of files when power failed on my computer by saving on USB.
*
*

Special talent

* Innovative fundraiser for Macmillan Cancer Support raising money selling cakes in school.
*
*

Remember the aim is to fit all the sentence on one line. This is what you're aiming for your chief skills section to look like. Now, let's put everything together that you have written. For your finished copy, you will not include the words I have in this format (e.g. your name, address, telephone, mobile, email, month, year, place, example etc.)

Your name
_____

Address   Telephone
                                           Mobile
                                           Email

Profile

Education and qualifications
Month   Year   Place

Key skills and abilities

Chief skill category 1
[Example]

[Example]

[Example]

Chief skill category 2
[Example]

[Example]

[Example]

Chief skill category 3
[Example]

[Example]

[Example]

Chief skill category 4
[Example]

[Example]

[Example]

Chief skill category 5
[Example]

[Example]

[Example]

Employment history or work experience (where relevant)
[As a reminder, list any full-time or part-time jobs you have had, beginning with the most recent. Include dates you were there, the job title and the name of the employer. If you haven't any, then list any work experience.]

Date   From   To   Position   Where   f/t p/t

Hobbies and interests

References (available on request)

Now it's time for you to have a go with what you have collected. Complete your CV structure with your chief skill examples.

Activity 5.2: Profile and evidence MOT

In order to write your profile so that it sounds snappy and punchy you have to think of action words that best describe you, your strengths, skills, characteristics, experience, abilities, capabilities. If you are still having difficulty thinking of some action words, then scan through the following list and use what you feel sums you up. Below I have brought together 161 words. Some may prove helpful when you're describing your skills, characteristic, attribute or ability.

acquired	described	enhanced
administered	designed	enlarged
affected	developed	ensured
applied	devised	eradicated
appointed	directed	established
approved	discovered	estimated
arranged	dismantled	evaluated
assembled	distinguish	exceeded
assessed	diversify	expanded
attained	diverted	experienced
broadened	documented	extended
built	doubled	finished
calculated	economical	formulated
changed	edited	founded
checked	effected	generalised
coordinated	efficient	generated
collated	eliminated	guided
collected	employed	identify
created	enacted	illustrated
critiqued	encouraged	implemented
defined	ended	improved
demonstrate	engineered	increased

initiated
inspected
inspired
installed
instigated
instructed
interpreted
introduced
invented
investigated
judged
justify
launched
led
lengthened
liaised
maintained
managed
manipulate
marketed
maximised
minimised
modernised
monitored
motivated
negotiated
obtained
operated
ordered
organised
outlined
participated

positive
prepare
presented
presided
prevented
processed
produced
productive
proficient
programmed
promoted
proved
provided
published
qualified
re-arranged
re-designed
re-directed
re-organised
re-structured
re-vamped
recall
recognised
recommended
recruited
rectified
reduced
regulated
reinforced
rejected
related
repaired

represented
reproduce
rescued
researched
resolved
resourceful
restored
retained
reviewed
revised
rewrite
separate
shaped
show
simplified
sold
specialised
specified
started
strengthened
structured
studied
successful
suggested
summarised
supported
taught
trained
transferred
undertook
write

Step Six

Polish It

Polishing is about making your principal CV shine and noticing if it is looking good. There are some very important things you have to look at when creating your CV. I mentioned some of these in Step 4 and now we are going to take a further look.

- Saving your principal CV;
- Spelling and grammar;
- Formatting margins;
- Spacing and layout;
- Font and size;
- Paper quality – if you're printing it out;
- Microsoft Word compatibility – if you're uploading it.

Saving your principal CV

I have written many times through this book, as this is your principal CV you will be using this as the original from which you can build all other CVs. When you're saving it, make sure you note that this is the principal one. You may have more than five chief skills – perhaps you decided to list more, that's fine, but remember, when you are submitting your CV for a job or work experience opportunity, to complete a target job profile and develop an overview of the skills and strengths they're seeking.

So save your principal CV like this:

CV Principal_2012_1

Then you can keep track of all other CVs.

Important hint
When saving in a Word document, you will notice that green grammar lines will appear if your sentences are quite punchy. This is why I would always save as a **PDF** when sending it via email or if you upload your CV. This way, your document will be read exactly as you want it.

Spelling

The spell-check will highlight any words that you may have overlooked. However, don't rely on it entirely. It is important to be consistent, for example with '-ise'/'-ize' words. A spell-checker may recognise both as acceptable spellings, but if you have spelled 'organize' with a 'z' in one line, and with an 's' a few lines further on, a prospective employer will not be impressed! Be guided by a good English dictionary and be consistent.

The more you check your work, giving yourself a few days in between, the more you will notice when words are misspelt. If you are showing your work to parents, tutors, siblings or friends, they will often notice spelling errors that you have missed.

Spelling is the first thing that potential recruiters will be looking for when they're casting their eyes over your CV.

Grammar

This is often a difficult nut to crack! You think a sentence sounds fine and then in your document you see it underlined in green, telling you that the spelling and grammar check doesn't like it. It could be that you need to move words around so that they flow and make better sense.

I would always recommend reading out loud. I know that may sound a tad 'primary school' but there's something in it. My mum, who's a poet and creative writer and in her mid 70s, always told me, as I was growing up, to read aloud **to hear** whatever I was writing. It sounds obvious but we tend to 'get it' when we read out loud. We hear the sentence differently.

When you're writing your evidence sentences and keeping them to one per line, this will be even more important for you.

Punctuation

This is an area that can either kill or save a sentence, and even though your sentences are going to be short and punchy, your commas and full stops have to be spot on.

Commas, full stops, dashes, colons and semi-colons are there for a reason and I read so many pieces of text that miss them out.

Why are they there? Well, they're used to ensure the reader pauses and breathes to digest what is being examined. They can separate different ideas within the same sentence. Reading out loud, again, can really help you 'feel' where there is a natural pause, or whether you've written something that is too long winded.

As a guide when you're compiling your evidence sentences, you can fit about 12–15 words on one line. This will obviously depend on your margins. Adding commas, semi-colons or colons will give an extra dimension. Shorter, punchier sentences can still convey a great deal of information.

Spelling, grammar and punctuation can often cause us to break into a sweat. With the ever-increasing use of text language, knowing when to use capital letters, begin new sentences and new paragraphs can all be a challenge. However, this is 'Polish it' and that means you can do just that, with a little more guidance from me. It's never the same when you're attempting to do this and you're on your own, so I will just do my best to explain it to you.

Now that you have this great fertile soil of your CV and you have something written down, you can relax a little and spend time on thinning and weeding.

Thesaurus

I find that I could not be without one. They just have to be one of the most useful tools in writing and can ensure you don't repeat the same words. In describing your skills and demonstrating your accomplishments, having the online Thesaurus open in your Word document can often just transform your sentence; you can also right-click on your highlighted word and check out 'synonyms'. If you have never really used a thesaurus, now would be a good time to do so.

Prepositions

Prepositions include such words as at, to, by, with, in, from etc. Ending a sentence with a preposition can be seen as pretty sloppy. However, there are times when ending a sentence this way is a much better way of phrasing, otherwise it can become very messy and the reader has no clue about what you're saying. For example, Winston Churchill once reportedly exclaimed, 'That is the sort of thing up with which I will not put!' to 'take the mickey' out of someone who criticised him for ending a sentence with a preposition ('That is the sort of thing I will not put up with').

If you change your evidence sentence to avoid ending with a preposition and it just adds to the confusion of what you were trying to say, then don't change it. Do keep this to a minimum though; you're doing your best to impress – if there's quite a number of sentences ending in prepositions, it may not read very well.

You may even find a few tucked away in this handbook – I hope not – but you never know!

Words

If you find you're still missing the right words, having difficulty describing some evidence or want to express yourself in more effective way, then go back to **Activity 5.2: Profile and**

evidence MOT, and you'll find a comprehensive list from A to Z, which may prove helpful to describe the examples you are giving for your skills and strengths.

Don't use words that you wouldn't normally use or that are unfamiliar to you. Feel comfortable about placing words in your sentences that describe and reflect what you're trying to say. Can you use any of the words to boost your sentences, your skills, experience, interests and accomplishments?

Circle the words that you think you could use – don't be tempted to pack your CV with too many of them as this can look completely out of place. A few subtle words to enhance your strengths can go a long way, but choose carefully and wisely. If you're unsure of the meaning, check in an online dictionary or a the hard copy version. Using some of these words will give your sentences clout and help you to avoid repetition.

When you are 'polishing' and you find that you're repeating yourself, make sure that you highlight what you believe is the most important example relevant to the category you're choosing. You will already have compiled your **target job profile**, a list of the skills and attributes describing the jobs you're seeking back in Step 2, so go back and double-check that you're citing an example that is relevant to that particular job description.

Formatting your page

Margins

These are often underused in a Word document but they can be incredibly useful, *especially when you need to fit your example on to one line.* When you open up a new Word document it will usually have set the margins and we always tend to use them without changing them. They are usually set at approximately 1 inch (25mm) all the way round: left, right, top, bottom. However, you do have the opportunity to slightly modify these.

Don't make the margins too narrow, but you certainly have the capacity to move them to give you more words to the page.

Why not see how it looks?

Font

It is very tempting to use the 'font of your dreams' in a CV and my creative side would say 'go for it'. However, it has to be legible and clear.

In the left-hand column of the box below, I have provided examples of the main fonts that you need to consider, while in the right-hand column you'll see those I wouldn't use for a CV (or expression statement).

Consider	Avoid
Arial	**Arial Black**
Calibri	Bradley Handwriting
Gill Sans	Comic Sans
Helvetica	Lucida Calligraphy
Tahoma	Marker Felt
Trebuchet MS	Papyrus
Verdana	Perpetua

I love fonts, I love the variety. However, for the purpose of creating your first CV, it's crucial to present a good impression.

Font size

When space is needed, your font can help! This is significant and often overlooked. The font size needs to be 11 or above but this can depend on the actual font you want to use. Don't go above 12, except if you are using it as a heading for your skill group.

For example: you can hopefully see from the following box that size 10 is just too small for this purpose.

Size 12	Size 11	Size 10
Arial	Arial	Arial
Calibri	Calibri	Calibri
Gill Sans	Gill Sans	Gill Sans
Helvetica	Helvetica	Helvetica
Tahoma	Tahoma	Tahoma
Trebuchet MS	Trebuchet MS	Trebuchet MS
Verdana	Verdana	Verdana

Activity 6.1: Here come the hints

1. Repetition

Are you repeating yourself because you want to fill a category space? If you are having difficulty thinking of three evidence examples, then think of just two. You don't have to fill up all of the space, remember it is quality not quantity. Check through your principal CV and see whether you are saying the same thing. You will be able to recognise this when you have spent a few days away from your text. When you read it with a fresh pair of eyes, you will notice if you are repeating yourself.

Decide which one sounds better and more professional, then delete the one that doesn't. If they both sound great, then you're just going to have to decide. Don't be tempted to put them both in. Ask someone.

If your chief skill categories are too similar and, consequently, your examples and evidence are too alike, start to consider other chief skills. Perhaps go back and insert a new skill group and provide a different range of examples.

2. Just describing

Do you start sentences with 'I have done this', 'I have done that'? Too much describing and not enough reflecting back on what you have *actually done* makes for a dull CV. If you have done something outstanding, then mention the particular details. Remember T-REX.

- Task
- Response
- Ending
- eXact

Expand on your accomplishment and spend time reflecting on what you have achieved and what is relevant to the chief skill. It's vitally important that you focus on the skill and always have your target job profile to hand.

3. Nicely does it

The word 'nice' or 'nicely' is great. I'm not personally attacking the word nice; I like it in fact. However, nice is a cover-up word for other lovely descriptive words. I find when I'm reading sentences with the word 'nice' in it they don't really say much. You may not use the word 'nice' in a sentence, that's fine, but if you have, I would suggest exploring other words that help to give more 'clout' to your information.

Read these and see what you think:

- I have a nice group of friends;
- I have developed my speaking skills nicely;
- The people are nice and friendly.

Bear in mind that if you do feel the urge to write 'nice', take a look at the thesaurus and find another word. I include examples below:

enjoyable	diverting	delightful
pleasant	lovely	engaging
agreeable	great	sympathetic
good	likeable	compassionate
satisfying	agreeable	good
gratifying	personable	courteous
delightful	amiable	civil
marvellous	affable	refined

| entertaining | friendly | polished |
| amusing | charming | elegant |

4. Feeling funny

Being humorous in words can sometimes backfire. You may feel it's relevant because you're going to send your CV to a creative job or opportunity, but think twice about adding humour. This can go either way for you – it may be received really well, but you're taking a risk. It would probably be more appropriate at the interview where facial expressions can be seen and the tone of your voice can be heard.

5. Are you really pitching to the job/experience/opportunity?

In creating your principal CV and using your newly-built target job profile, you will be explaining your commitment, interest and enthusiasm by showing examples of how you're meeting the requirements. However, be sure to have completed your TJP, as you do need to know what skill requirements they're seeking.

If you're struggling for words and themes, you can revisit some of the activities to repeat again. That's where you go to rediscover some inspiration.

6. How far back do you go when writing examples and evidence?

Make sure that whatever you're writing is relevant. If you're highlighting a primary school experience, it will have to be quite applicable (even stupendous!) to the skill you're talking about. Perhaps this is too far back. Employers want to read about recent activity so I would suggest you look at the previous 3–4 years maximum. If you're an adult returner then you still have great scope to reflect upon and you can go back to wherever you feel is relevant to support your five chief skills.

Activity 6.2: Bring on the feedback

Now is the time to release your principal CV to family, friends, tutors, or colleagues for their feedback. It is always important to receive feedback, but only do this if you are ready to share. You will hopefully receive some good comments that will highlight strengths and weaknesses and you'll probably find that it is related to your grammar and how you have written your evidence statements.

It is crucial to ask for comments from people who teach you or coach you, as they're used to reading CVs and they're not caught up in the emotion of writing. They will be the best people to pick up spelling errors and grammar mishaps and by revealing your CV so far, you will show them how much you have accomplished.

Step Seven

Complete It

Only when you are *really happy* with your CV do you consider 'Complete it', meaning you think it's ready to sign off and send off. You could now be taking it to an educational advisor to check, or a mentor to advise and assess. This is different from feedback from family or friends. Whenever you think you're at the point of completing it, then here's where I offer you the 4 Rs to give you a little more breathing space.

The 4 Rs: reflect, rejig, refine and reassure

Reflect

Simply put, reflect means sit back and review, not only with yourself but also, perhaps a tutor, mentor or advisor; it's time to double check that all the necessary components of the CV are present and correct. This is not just about the CV but also about the other section, such as the covering letter. Have you checked it all for errors? This is the time to reflect. I have used this word a fair amount in this book, so what does it mean?

To reflect: we can understand the word 'reflect' in the following ways.

- To send something back: *the moon reflects light from the sun towards the earth.*

- To think seriously: *this will give us time to reflect.*

- To say something to yourself thoughtfully: *I reflected that leaving might be the safest option.*

If you read through your CV giving yourself time to reflect, saying those sentences to yourself, quietly, or even involving a close friend or confidante and reading it back to them, you will engage with your skill groups and examples in a different way. Sometimes we battle on, just on our own and all we need to do is sit back, involve others whom we trust and re-read our words.

This time of reflection is just that.

Rejig

Are there any last minute rejigs needed? What do I mean by rejig? The word jig we know is a type of dance, a skip, hop and a spring. To rejig, according to the *Concise Oxford English Dictionary*, means to rearrange, so here I'm asking you: do your evidence sentences need to be rearranged? Are there words that need to hop into other sentences? Are they flowing?

You can still move things around. Ensure there's a flow with the skill categories; it's not too late. Now is the time to be really confident about what you've written. Be realistic and if you have too much content, you have to remove words. If you overflow on lines and can't fit it all in neatly, then you may need to reduce these words. Don't get attached to words, or sentences. Make changes.

Look at all the small words that make up the sentence. Do you need them all? Are you repeating yourself in the categories? Are your examples all different?

In your reflection, you may have underlined text to rejig. Go on, move things around! See if things read better in a different order.

This is the time to play with your structure and see how it reads. Often when we start with one way, we need to just change things around and read them back in a different way. That's why I've called it 'rejig' because it is a 'dance' – a playful dance of words.

Refine

Refine is about improving any words that you feel aren't selling you. Take time to check through them with the thesaurus and confirm that you've used the correct word. Don't feel you have to cramp all your chief skills together, it won't look professional and it's difficult to read. You may also find that you remove certain words during this 'refine' phase.

Reassure

This really needs to read 'be reassured'. Reassured by whom? By yourself. It's important that you feel confident that you have created a good quality CV that you believe promotes your enthusiasm and skills and conveys to the recruiter what your experiences are and how you have developed and demonstrated them.

Your advisor or mentor – whoever this may be – connected to your school, college or place of work, may be able to reassure you. Your mentor must be someone who can support you through this process. Some of us can write CVs quickly and without too much stress (although I'm not convinced). However, a great many individuals become concerned and struggle with the blank page, so it's necessary to be reassured by your mentor.

Be reassured that when you finally pass this to an advisor, mentor or referee for checking there won't be any surprises for them and they will be fully supportive of your evidence. It's important that you have this backing.

Be reassured that you've done the best you could possibly do, you have researched and analysed your chief skills and provided good examples and you're happy with what you have written. Now all you have to do is wait to hear you have been invited for interview.

Congratulations! You have created your first ever CV in seven easy steps.

Explore your network

Now it's time to **explore your network** and uncover who may be around you. Don't forget that 'people know people who know people'.

It is a well-known fact that people find jobs via people they know in their network, their circle. It is the age-old business of referrals and it is a sure-fire way of finding a part-time job, temporary summer work, work experience, volunteering or even a full-time permanent job. Now that you have your principal CV you can start to promote yourself by finding people who are in your network. It is now all about investigating your network.

You have a core group that will be in your network. Look at your mobile phone contacts or your Facebook profile and see how many individuals you have as 'friends'. What's the estimate? If you extend this by looking at the friends of friends, you enter an even bigger network. Those acquainted with you through a mutual friend can be a real asset when you're aiming for a job opportunity or work experience. You may be thinking 'Why or how can these people help me?'

Sometimes we really don't know who is available and who could perhaps assist us with finding prospective work. We have a set of friends but do we know what their parents do or in which industry they are based? The next activity gives you some space to think about who are your core friends, providing you with the chance to list them and then find out what their parents/relatives do. In taking your first ever CV to the next level, this would be my very first port of call – these would be the people to seek out and send/email your CV, having researched their industry and realised it could be an ideal opportunity for you.

For this next activity, go through your list of friends, your mobile contacts and also your parents' friends and their mobile phone contacts, Facebook friends or LinkedIn contacts.

A prime example of this working is where year 11 student Greg came to me wanting to find part-time work. We talked about his network, especially through his dad who owns his own business, belongs to a business referral organisation and has a key circle of contacts. One of these contacts had a suitable job for Greg and asked him to email his CV. Greg didn't have one ready yet. Perhaps he missed an opportunity? The point is that there was a whole circle of contacts who were available via his dad and, therefore, this would be the first place to start by providing your CV to an already existing network of contacts that 'know of you'. That's the *key* here – they 'know' you via a family member or friend.

Activity 7.1: Know your network

1. Go through your mobile contacts and your friends list on Facebook, making a note of friends about whom you feel confident and comfortable enough to approach to find out what their parents do. (You may already know what their parents do.) Remember there are also relatives of these friends, and these must be people whom you feel you could approach. You can always build upon this at a later stage. Also note any contacts from your own extended family. These people are your inner circle in your network of contacts.

2. Now let's move to your next level circle of contacts. Write down the names of the contacts you have discovered who are connected to people from your inner circle, or friends of friends. This may also be a place for people in the community whom you know, teachers, advisors, or coaches.

3. There is also another level where you can contact friends of friends of friends – someone who has been referred to you.

The purpose of this activity is to take the time to think about the people *already around you*. This is always the first place to begin. Although we always feel we need to start with job adverts, we perhaps may have someone closer to home.

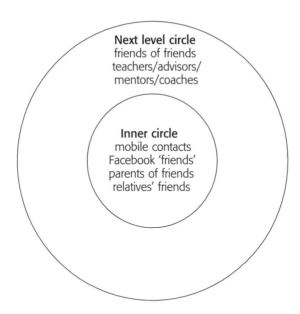

When I was 17, I got a temporary summer job in an office. I found this job through a friend of a family friend. I had sent them my CV and covering letter and was lucky enough to get an interview. Back then it was a really basic CV. It wasn't based on any skills. So I was lucky. If I hadn't asked around my friends, I would never have found it. The contacts that I made from that job enabled me to get more temporary summer work in following years. So it starts with just one job and you can then build upon it for future roles. It may not be the ideal job and exactly what you want to do, but it will be building your skill base. As one of the employers in my circle told me:

> *Networking and making yourself (however shy!) chat to lots of different people is important. Young people need to find out about jobs, what people do, what they enjoy, and get themselves known and liked in the workplace. Being lovely and friendly and offering to make people coffee and do their photocopying, although it may feel demeaning, shows people you aren't too big for your boots and are happy to muck in which is always a likeable trait and may sometimes lead to something.*
>
> Employer, Museum of Liverpool

If you have friends who are employed, you could ask them whether

- they like their jobs;
- how they got them;
- whether there are any job openings.

If you can, gather all the information they give you and perhaps they might also put in a good word for you.

> **Using any friends and contacts in your circle gives you the best chance of landing a job.**

We hear people say that it is harder to find a job if you don't have much work experience but it takes hard work to find a job no matter how old you are.

Putting your CV on a job site and then sitting back to wait for a hit is the wrong approach. You need to do everything you can to find the job or work opportunity, and creating a CV that sells your skills is the first foundation layer.

That's why networking, looking at job opportunities online, via job boards, for example Gumtree (www.gumtree.com); studying companies you love, plus having mock interviews are all ingredients for this mixture.

Part Two
Where to Start with Covering Letters and Application Forms

Writing Covering Letters

The days have long gone when people traipsed round city centres with copies of beautifully printed CVs, dropping them off to a shop, business or organisation. If you're under 20, then you probably won't even know that this happened. Nowadays, we have the luxury of email but that doesn't make it easier, it just means you have to be more focused and direct with your approach.

Simply handing or sending a CV in without any introductory letter is not a good first impression. In Part Two, I want to introduce you to creating a covering letter that will present you in a positive light and, hopefully, secure an invitation to an interview. At this stage, that is all you are seeking.

When starting to write a covering letter you will need the exact details of the recipient. Who are you addressing in the letter? What's their name, their position in the company? Have you got the correct address?

There are two types of covering letters:

1. Sending one for a job that is being advertised.
2. Sending one speculatively to ask for a job, voluntary work, a shadowing opportunity or work experience. (Take another look at **Activity 7.1: Know your network** as you could be sending it to someone you know via a referral.)

All the information you will include in a covering letter is already contained in your CV. You are not reinventing the wheel but highlighting some of the points you have introduced in your CV. All the activities that you have completed throughout this book will be useful to include in a covering letter; the profile, the flows, chief skills and evidence sentences. If you have followed the activities and completed a TJP, you will have a clear idea of the skills that the company/organisation is seeking. If there isn't a specific job role available, but you have found something that is comparable, you will notice the skills and knowledge that are similar. Consequently, in a covering letter, you can give examples of your own experiences, which will match the criteria they need.

Sometimes individuals think that they can use one template for a covering letter and be done with it. It still takes time and effort to tailor your covering letter to accompany your CV. A good cover letter can be a great signpost for an employer, actively encouraging them to spend more time reading your CV. So it is worth the effort.

Don't rush it – whether you're uploading, emailing or sending a hard copy – why would you spend time creating and perfecting your CV and then rush the covering letter? Most importantly, the first step is to find out who will be the recipient of your letter. What is their name and job title? It will be looked upon favourably if you have taken the time to find out the person's name and title rather than just writing Dear Sir/Madam, which is pretty impersonal.

The structure of a covering letter

As I have mentioned earlier there are two types of covering letters:

1. applying for a job that is advertised;
2. applying 'on spec'.

The letter needs to be about four or five small paragraphs of about four or five lines each and take up no more than a single A4 page. If you're applying for a job that is advertised, then paragraph one must contain why you are applying and what you have to offer, making sure it is relevant to the job. (This is where the TJP is useful.)

In paragraph two mention how your skills, experience and

achievements are related to the person specification of the job. This is where you can refer them to your chief skills and highlight some examples of evidence. If you're writing on spec then you will need to show that you have researched the company. You can write a paragraph describing why you would like to work for that company and what sort of role you're looking for in that organisation.

A covering letter that looks as though it's regurgitated is not going be very impressive. Anything that shows you have done research about the company is a plus.

In concluding the letter, don't forget to thank the reader for their time spent reading your words and for considering the application. Be up front and say you would be interested in the opportunity to meet them for an interview.

Don't just repeat what is on your CV: you have the capacity to reintroduce the 'itsy bitsy' words and expand a little more.

Below you will find a sample covering letter template: I'm not normally a fan of templates, so this is really just a guide for structure and layout.

Note
Some employers tell me they really like to receive a handwritten covering letter as this shows your personality and individuality. The template below would still be used if you decided to write instead of type.

Address

Email

Mobile

Date

Name of recipient
Position in company
Company address

Dear Mr or Mrs.............

Application for ....
[Insert job title if the job is advertised, otherwise just put your name.]

Please find enclosed my CV in support of my application for the post of
.... in........................
Or

Please find enclosed my CV for you to consider. I am currently seeking part-time/full-time*work/a short spell of work experience*/voluntary work* with your company/organisation.
*[*Delete where necessary.]*

Paragraph 1: *[Why am I applying to them? What interests me about the type of job or the company? What do I have to offer them. Make sure it is relevant to the job description that I have developed in the TJP.]*

I am applying for this job because............

Paragraph 2: *[Take my profile from my CV and use some of the sentences to introduce the kind of person I am and the skills/abilities I have.]*

As you can see from my profile, I am............

Paragraph 3: *[How are my skills, experience and achievements related to the person specification of the job? Look at the TJP and chief skills and choose examples from my Principal CV to highlight how I have done something similar. Give them some examples here of my evidence.]*

I pride myself on the following chief skills............The evidence shows that my skills are easily transferred to other work settings and situations.

Paragraph 4: *[Tell them the kind of role I am looking for in their company/organisation and why I feel I have the skills to do it.]*

As I am seeking full or part time work, *a work experience for two weeks, voluntary work with your company/organisation*. I know a little about the roles you offer within your company and I believe that............
*[*Delete where necessary and name the organisation.]*

Paragraph 5: *[Show that I have researched the company, explain to them that I understand their mission. Summarise why I would like to work for this company.]*

I would like to work for your company because...........

Paragraph 6: Conclusion.
[Thank them for taking the time to consider my CV and application (if this is for a specific job). Don't just repeat verbatim what is on my CV, I can reintroduce the 'itsy bitsy' words and expand a little more.]

Thank you very much for taking the time to read and consider my CV and application. I would be very interested to meet with you for an interview, where, hopefully, I can show you how my knowledge and skills are easily transferable.

I look forward to hearing from you.

Yours sincerely
[This is to be used if you have the exact name of the recipient of the letter. If you're addressing it to Dear Sir/Madam, you will sign off with Yours faithfully.]

Insert your name
[Don't forget to sign with a pen if you're printing and sending via post. If this is online application, why not create a scanned signature and insert it here.]

Type your name

Completing Application Forms

More and more employers are requesting a completed application form – this is becoming the main way they recruit. If you have read through all the information in this book about person specifications, essential and desirable criteria, created your own target job profile and provided proof and evidence for your chief skills: I can safely say that you will be at an advantage when it comes to completing an application form. All of these activities have been included specifically to build your confidence.

It is essential to make sure you read through all of the application form and follow the guidelines that they provide. Don't veer off and do your own thing.

If they ask you not to include a CV, then don't. If they say you can continue onto another sheet for the expression statement, use only one extra page, don't add reams.

Time management

I would suggest that you don't leave it till the last minute to submit your application, even if it is online. Technology has its own rhythm and can be problematic; it may just cause undue stress and worry if it's not working just when you need to hit the send button.

If you're printing it out, make sure you have enough ink in your printer cartridges.

Write in all the available spaces

Potential employers tell me that many applicants do not make use of the maximum words allowed and write just one or two sentences in the area that asks: 'Why do you think you will be suitable for this job?' They tell me that good communication, common sense and good listening are strong skills that they will seek from a candidate. They will look for relevance as to why you are applying to that particular company/organisation, so it is important to show that you have an interest. This may seem obvious, but I'm told that candidates often leave out this very basic fact. For example, an employer said to me that candidates applying to be a police cadet often omitted writing about their interest in police work or that they're studying a course connected to the legal profession, e.g. law.

Writing Expression Statements within Application Forms

I am going to share the best tip I ever learnt about completing expression statements.

Earlier, when you created a target job profile, you will have been referring to a person specification provided with the job (if there isn't one, you will hopefully have found something similar).

In writing a statement of expression, instead of compiling evidence and proof for your CV, you need to provide evidence that relates exactly to the person specification that they have provided.

As you will have seen, categories are grouped together. For example, knowledge, skills/abilities and personal attributes. If these are provided with the job description and application form, then you provide evidence statements just like you did for your chief skills. Only this time, the headings you will have are headings required by the company/organisation.

The best tip I ever learnt was to *include the headings within my expression statement*. These show the criteria you're addressing and will make it easier for the recruiter to read and begin the shortlisting process. I have assessed countless statements that relate to specific criteria and it is the one thing that individuals miss out. All the text is often provided in one mass and the criteria are not clearly defined. As a potential recruiter and assessor, I am looking for examples and evidence to show me that you have done something similar or transferable. Break up the text with the headings and group the criteria together. This will create a far easier document to read and it will keep you on track so that you don't miss anything out. It also will prevent you jumping back and forth and not having any flow to your statement.

Tip

When starting your application form, save a copy for draft use and to practise on. A suggestion would be to print out the application and familiarise yourself with the questions – writing notes and guiding points on each relevant question. Don't forget to save/print a copy of your completed application before sending it off.

Part Three
Interviews: You've Got One!

How to Prepare for an Interview

You've got an interview! Well done. This is wonderful news.

When I'm working with clients, advice for interviews is always featured somewhere in our sessions. Even if you aren't being called for an interview soon, it is still worthwhile reading this chapter now and re-read it when you are attending an interview.

I have put together this section to help you get through interview preparation, the interview itself and après interview.

Remember the 5 Ps – this I believe, was/is an army phrase: Proper | Preparation | Prevents | Poor | Performance.

The preparation: You have the date and time to attend; now you have to reacquaint yourself with the following:

- company/organisation;
- job description;
- employee specification;
- target job profile that you compiled for this job;
- your CV and covering letter;
- your five chief skills and examples;
- the venue you need to attend;
- travel details;
- what you'll wear.

In the hope that you spent a good amount of time on **Step 1 – Gather It** and **Step 2 – Develop It**, you will probably find that you have a great deal of research material written down. One thing you have at your disposal is *your CV*, and the *covering letter* you wrote. You also have the *target job profile* that you created which will remind you of the key strengths, skills abilities and knowledge that this job requires.

Now you have to re-read what you wrote, asking yourself these questions:

- What was it about the job opportunity that I liked?
- What did I find interesting about the job?
- What do I know about the company/organisation?
- How do my skills and strengths match those that they're asking for?

Spend time revisiting the company/organisation website to refresh your memory. Review the target job profile – it's all there from when you did your initial research, but now, you could be talking 3–4 months later. (This will depend how keen you were in getting your CV created and how long they took to respond.)

I would suggest making some new notes about the company/ organisation where you will be interviewed; I'm allocating some fresh clean space here to jot down your notes about the job, the place and the type of person they're seeking. If you already have some notes that you think will be relevant, perhaps copy them down here, so you can now focus on the interview.

New notes:

Your previous notes:

Have you been sent information about your interview or was this invitation over the telephone? Find out as much as you can about the interview, as this will help you. Talk to anybody you know who may have been to a job interview.

Even if you don't know anyone who has had a job interview before, chat to heads of sixth form or careers advisors. They will have supported previous candidates.

Mock interviews

If you can I would suggest having a mock interview with a teacher or careers advisor, preferably someone you don't know very well. If you can't arrange this due to circumstances, then I'd suggest you have a chat with someone who could help you with questions to ask as well as plan some answers. Often interviewers will ask you things such as:

- What subjects do you enjoy most at school/college?
- What attracted you to this job opportunity?
- What are you reading at the moment?
- What are you following in the news?
- What would you say are your strengths?
- What would be something you wish to develop?
- Can you give me an example of working in a team to achieve a task?
- Can you work on your own, without supervision? When have you done this?
- Can you tell me anything about this company/organisation?

Therefore, in your preparation, make sure you note down the reasons behind why you applied for that job, what attracted you to the job (include things from the job description). Remember to print off your target job profile that you developed for this job and also to re-create a new one in www.wordle.net if you need to do so.

Whatever you mentioned in your CV and covering letter could be discussed at an interview, so familiarise yourself with what you have written.

I interviewed a client recently who just sat on her hands as she thought that she moved them too much. What sitting on the hands does is hunch the shoulders, which made her seem slouchy. Had she just been herself and used her hands in the normal way she might have felt more relaxed.

Mock interviews will highlight any idiosyncrasies you may have and a run-through with a couple of people will be very important in making you aware of these. What mock interviews or run-throughs provide is a dress rehearsal. Although you can't predict the conversation, you can prepare for the feelings it evokes. You wouldn't expect anyone not to practise before they went on stage to perform or ran the 100 metres. It then doesn't feel so new when you get to the real thing.

Being asked about work experience in an interview

I suggest keeping a journal when you're completing any work experience. In fact, I always recommend having a journal anyway. I don't mean keeping a diary of the sort that just records short snappy facts every day; I'm talking about a journal.

You don't have to write reams and reams, but it is worthwhile noting down specific incidents or experiences that you have encountered and learning opportunities. Often we just don't remember these times when we need to and it could be beneficial at this stage, because then you can bring such experiences to the interview. That can be impressive, especially if you are asked how you coped with a stressful situation at work. You may not have a massive work history time line, but you will have had stressful situations that you had to overcome.

Re-read your CV and covering letter

This may sound obvious but re-read your CV and the covering

letter because it's important to review what you wrote. I always advise applicants to print off a copy of their CV and covering letter as well as the target job profile and to keep it handy so that they can scan through it while they're sitting waiting to be called. This also applies to any extra interview notes you have made about the company. The bigger the picture you can paint about them, the more you will impress them that you have researched them and know exactly what you're embarking upon. You could even contemplate taking this book with you as it can often just jog your memory when you need it most. Hopefully, by this point this book is written in, doodled in and feeling completely 'yours'.

Remember they're not just interviewing you. You're asking questions too.

An important area that is often overlooked is being up to date with current affairs, and specifics within the industry/sector you're applying to. I can give an example of a client, let's call her Sarah, who went for an interview for a retail store; the interviewer asked Sarah about her favourite designers and the trends she was following at major fashion shows and exhibitions, plus she was also curious to know which magazines Sarah was reading.

Although Sarah knew what she wanted to answer, as this was her first interview since attending secondary school (i.e. seven years previously) she panicked; she hadn't really prepared the answers and made a blanket statement. The interviewer knew it too. If she had researched a little more, making some background notes about the fashion industry, she could have pulled something topical out of her hat and impressed the interviewer by talking about something that was current.

Some candidates are naturally very good at doing this, but this comes with confidence about your own ability. For the majority of people, it takes preparation and research. So don't think you have to develop a photographic memory, just a collection of notes can often provide a point of reference in a tight situation.

I believe it's important to follow the news. Not the doom and gloom news on the TV, but you can now be extremely selective via the web and zoom on the industry/field that interests you.

Preparing questions

My coaching clients ask me about preparing questions to ask the interviewer because people often find this daunting. Asking questions at interview shows that you're engaged with the company/organisation, you're interested in them and want to seek more facts from them.

You may find that when researching for the previous stages, questions have popped up and you've recorded them. If they haven't, now's a good time to think about what further information you'd like regarding this job. You don't have to think of these things on your own: seek advice and guidance from those around you.

The interview

Employers don't generally invite you to an interview so they can catch you out. They genuinely want to meet you and they know it's a nervous business. It's pointless for them to invite you and then set you up to fail. It's OK for you to ask them to repeat a question if you need a little extra time to think about the answer, or you don't understand what they say, but don't do that all through the interview. Don't be put off by interviewers writing notes as you're speaking, they may be seeing quite a number of candidates and they need to differentiate between you and the others. The more they scribble down may mean that you have said something that they like. Obviously it could be the other way round, but often they just want to record your thoughts so that when they all meet again to make a selection, they have a reference to you.

The venue

Have all the venue details to hand and know how you're going to get there, don't leave it till 10.30pm the night before. If you're being taken there, make sure your driver knows all the details, print off anything that may help with the journey, don't leave it to them to organise.

If you're travelling by public transport then book your ticket in advance (if need be), check and double check your times so you are not rushing to get there. It all adds to the stress of the preparation if it is last minute. I'm sure you have all of this sorted and organised. If not, then this can act as a reminder and a small nudge forward.

Finally (and you know this anyway), get an early night.

Visualising success

There's a great deal to be said for visualising success before it happens. See yourself feeling confident, walking in, making good eye contact and answering the questions clearly and with enthusiasm.

Athletes practise visualisation and have done so for many years, business coaches also work this way with their clients. You have to see what you want to see, hear what you want to hear and then feel what you want to feel. This can calm your nerves because, in a way, you've walked through the process in your mind before visiting in person.

Have you ever tried visualisation? Let's give it a go now, here's how.

Interview visualisation

It can be done at any time when you have five minutes to shut your eyes and sit still, without any distractions. Turn off your mobile and close your laptop. What I sometimes suggest is reading this passage through into your mobile phone and then play it back to yourself when you need to focus on the positive outcome of your interview.

Remember to read it slowly, pause over the words as if you were guiding somebody else through it and delete anything that isn't really relevant. It's up to you.

Visualise the location, where you're going and what you're wearing. You don't have to know the exact location, as you probably haven't visited before. See yourself waking up on the morning of the interview, ten minutes before your alarm is due to go off – your body clock is in sync with you. Eat breakfast if you normally do (but I'd suggest even if you don't eat breakfast that you have something to ground you – a banana, piece of toast, a smoothie).

Before you get out of bed, see yourself calmly walking through your day in your mind; your clothes are all ready and laid out the night before, you're happy with your decision; your clothes are freshly ironed; you did it all yesterday. You've got everything ready in a bag with your research material and you're fully confident that you know where you'll be travelling.

See yourself taking the journey, whether you're driving or taking public transport. You know where you're going; you have all the maps and telephone numbers should you need them. You get a seat on the bus/train, you're comfortable in your car and there's an effortless flow of traffic. Find your parking space, see yourself arriving, no fluster whatsoever, you are at least 30 minutes before your allotted time which gives you the opportunity to find your bearings, take a breather, walk round the area, locate the room, know where you're heading and sit down for a few minutes. You arrive at the reception for the allotted time and introduce yourself; you take a seat and wait to be called into the interview room.

As you sit calmly, you read over your notes, you look at the target job profile, re-read your five chief skills and individual evidence and you refresh your thoughts and questions. A member of the panel approaches you, you stand, shake hands, calmly introduce yourself and smile. Best foot forward, you confidently walk with them to the interview room. You get my gist?

It's good to see the whole process in your mind. I used to do this when I was delivering training programmes and travelling all over the UK. I would see myself driving there, arriving the night before if need be, finding the location smoothly, setting up the space, meeting people, calmly, confidently and feeling suitably watered and comfortably fed. I would walk through the day in my mind in any quiet moments I had, especially when I was just starting out and feeling apprehensive about delivering to a different group of clients. If you feel up for it, give it a go. You will surprise yourself, I'm sure.

On the day of the interview

Listen to the questions and take a breath, don't feel pressured or try to guess what they want for an answer. Waffling is a sign you've gone off the point of the question, this comes with experience so don't worry too much about this – the interviewer will be aware of nerves and 'waffling tendencies'. They're going to be looking for your interest in the job and they want to know you can show your skills and strengths are transferable. They want to hear about your skills and your evidence. They know you haven't had much work history – they have invited you to an interview knowing all this, so it is up to you to refer to all your evidence and examples that you have spent time gathering.

In most cases, interviewers want to see that you have the potential. Allow your enthusiasm to flow.

Body language and non-verbal communication

Be aware of body language and make eye contact with your interviewers. If there is more than one interviewer – make eye contact with *all* of them as you talk. If you're concerned about body language and your own non-verbal communications then there are reference texts about body language and communication skills.

Listening to questions

Listening carefully to questions is something that is important and often overlooked, as interviews are normally all about preparing the answers.

Have you ever found yourself in a situation when your mind is really not on the question because you're busy thinking about the answer after you've heard the first few words? Then you forget the second part of the question they were asking. I have been in this situation quite a number of times as I have a tendency to jump ahead in my mind. Maybe you do too.

There's no right answer to this one as with experience this improves. However, if you have run through interviews in role-play, that's where you gain the practice. Notice how you listen to other questions in your life. Do you jump in before the entire question has been asked? Are you pre-empting what the question is going to be? Bear this in mind when you're attending an interview.

Completing the interview

Finishing the interview can be a relief and you will probably want to just rush out as fast as you can. I'm with you on that one. It's liberating to have finished so be sure you stay positive right until the end, even though you may want the ground to open up and swallow you whole because you think you've done really badly. Remember that's not always how it seems to the interviewer.

We are often extremely tough on ourselves. When we think we've done very badly we have often done pretty well. So maintain that professional and positive air before you leave the room and if you can, complete the process with a handshake.

I really hope that you're successful with your job interview, whether this is for part-time or full-time work, maybe a volunteering job you really wanted, or a work experience for four weeks. Don't be disheartened if you don't get it.

Get back on the bike and carry on cycling!

Part Four
Hints from Employers
and Frequently Asked Questions
(FAQs)

Hints from Employers

Merseyside Police

Spelling and grammar will always be analysed, in particular the use of wrong words, spelling or grammatical errors. We will be looking out for:

- missing capital letters and full stops;
- over-long sentences;
- sentences that do not make sense or are incomplete.

Has the applicant explained why they want the job with us, either full time, part time, or work experience? It may seem obvious – but state why you're writing and what you're hoping to achieve.

Has the applicant explained what skills they have?

Has the applicant explained what they hope to achieve on the placement/job?

Have they just sent a CV without a covering letter? If so, it tends not to be read, unless we had specified this fact.

Museum of Liverpool

First of all, covering letters need to be short, well designed and used to highlight the pertinent points on a CV or application form.

Every employer needs to read about good communication skills and administrative skills. Young people need to build on admin and IT skills and any kind of voluntary experience which involves working with the public. What I would say is go easy on the amount of voluntary work they do – one day a week of relevant voluntary experience is more valuable when combined with a decent temping job, however far removed it may seem from where they want to be. Full-time voluntary work may not necessarily make them that employable.

Roy Castle Lung Foundation

I do think that CVs are relevant today – they give you an overview of the person, allowing you a brief insight into their skill base/experience, etc. However, I would state that sometimes they can become very clinical and too brief with no warmth or personal content in them – so I also like to see either a personal statement or a covering letter. If they add more detail in the covering letter about their personality, why they would want to work with you, what they could bring – that stands out.

I look closely at the first couple of pages, after that if the person has not captured me, then I do begin to lose interest. Depending on how many CVs I receive, I probably spend a couple of minutes and definitely prefer no more than three pages in total.

I want the personal statement and covering letter to stand out, giving me a little insight into the type of person they are – for example, their transferable skills – their ability to communicate/ sell themselves.

Transferable skills that I seek are: commitment (understanding of what commitment is); flexibility; communication, and I think in this current environment the willingness to embrace change, a positive 'can do' attitude.

I do like to read skills-based CVs. If no evidence is available how could they be able to match the criteria?

I want to tell people with limited work experience that I think the most important thing is to get across that they are flexible, they are keen to work, they would be very committed to the role, and they are looking to develop themselves.

Charitable Organisation – Open Door Association La Porte Ouverte (France)

CVs are still relevant. It gives the interviewer information with which to question the applicant in greater detail and helps highlight the applicant's qualities and interests as well as their educational attainments.

I spend as long as it requires if it is interesting and well presented. Rather like a book or play it has to have a good beginning to grab my interest and make me want to read more about the applicant. It is in my interest to devote as much time as possible to reading a CV, as the financial investment in each employee is considerable. If I can present a good and varied shortlist for any vacancy my investment will not be in vain and will soon reap rewards.

Difficult to say how long a CV needs to be – how long is a piece of string? Seriously, say what you have to say in the most precise and positive way.

I want the interests and experiences of the applicant to stand out when I'm reading a CV. Assuming that the applicant possesses the educational qualifications required for the post then his/her interests and experiences would make the applicant stand out over other applicants with the same or similar qualifications.

If you're attempting to get work experience with little or no work history, my advice would be – undertake as many experiences as you can, which can demonstrate your reliability, trustworthiness, ability and positive attitude.

I will read a covering letter, particularly if it is hand written and I would want it to show literacy skills and positivity in highlighting one or two parts of the CV that are applicable to the vacancy on offer, particularly in the area of the applicant's personal qualities. If the CV has a large amount of content, then the covering letter may also highlight to me any qualifications and experiences that are relevant to the position available. I have in the past offered a position to somebody who may have not been as well qualified as their rivals, but a light shone through them and their presentation and I was prepared to take a chance on them.

Don't be tempted to waffle and stretch the truth in either your CV or covering letter.

My thanks go to my employers circle who contributed to answering a few of my questions.

Frequently Asked Questions (FAQs)

■ **I have sent my CV and covering letter and haven't heard anything from them. What shall I do?**

We often think we have to sit back and just wait, hoping to hear that we have an interview. Right?

My experience shows that if you carry on waiting to hear a response, you could be waiting a long time. This can be quite soul destroying so I would always suggest the following things to consider:

If you have sent your CV and covering letter 'on spec'.
'On spec' means there is no job that you're specifically applying for but you have decided to pitch your strengths, skills and abilities to a particular company/organisation. You may have been given the name of a manager or a coordinator and you felt it would be in your best interests to send them your CV and covering letter.

When this is the case, I would advise leaving it for a couple of weeks. If you haven't heard anything by then, this would be a good time to telephone them and find out if they received it and if they have had the time to review it. Sometimes, the response from these phone calls is not that positive, but what it does do is 'take the control back to you'. You can then make a note that it's unlikely that you will hear from them, or likely you will hear. Whatever the outcome, you can then move on to the next job/opportunity.

Tick them off and move on.

If you have sent your CV and covering letter in response to a job advert, work experience or volunteering opportunity.

When applying for a job role, part/full time or volunteering opportunity it is important to note down in your file when the deadline is for submission. This is often included in the job information – usually something like this:

If you haven't heard back from us within six weeks after the closing date, then unfortunately you have not been successful on this occasion. We thank you very much for submitting your CV and hope that you are successful in finding further work opportunities.

It is difficult to know what to do if you haven't heard within six weeks. You want to hear **something**, from **someone** – a human response, to say 'Thank you for applying, sorry you haven't been successful'. What I would suggest (and if you feel confident in doing so) would be to contact the company and explain that this is your first time doing anything like this and you would find some feedback really helpful.

They may respond and give you feedback on your CV or covering letter, or they may choose not to answer you, but at least you are asking the right questions.

It is often difficult receiving feedback for a job where you haven't been interviewed, but the times that I have done so, it has always proved helpful.

It is definitely more beneficial to ask for feedback if you have been interviewed but unfortunately were not successful. You will be gleaning information that is related to your interview style.

Tip
I would always recommend getting feedback from employers and organisations – especially as this is the first (or nearly first) time when you have applied for something. You can learn so much from their reaction and reply.

- **Can I stretch the truth a bit on my CV?**
  There's a difference between selling yourself and inventing things. Selling yourself is putting your skills and experience in the best light. Never be tempted to invent qualifications or previous jobs. You might be asked for more information about them at the interview stage. More importantly, don't be tempted at any time to copy any text from any CVs or expression statements you have found online. If invited to an interview you will be expected to answer questions based on what you have written.

- **If I'm sending my CV, should I print it back-to-back?**
  I would only print on separate pieces of paper. Do not print on both sides of the paper.

- **Can I be creative and design my own template?**
  As you've seen from the book, information does need to be laid out simply, clearly and in an easy-to-read format. It is vital that all the essential information is instantly visible. Headings are necessary – this will then ensure that any potential employer can see straight away what he/she wants to read. Avoid fancy headers, footers, page numbers, borders, title pages, binders or covers.

- **Shall I include the words curriculum vitae at the beginning of my CV?**
  It is obvious to anyone reading what it is, so no, it's not necessary.

- **What do recruiters really dislike on a CV?**
  If you have watched *The Apprentice* and seen the interview phase, one thing they really dislike is *inaccurate dates*. Make sure you put the right dates down and explain any gaps in education or examinations. This also means inaccurate contact details – you have created your CV so that you will get an interview so make sure you have all the correct details on it. This may seem obvious but people make mistakes.

The job description and employee specification tell you what the employer requires. If you don't have those skills or attributes, employers may feel that you're not being serious about the job – so ensure that you are pitching to the job, at the right level for you.

■ **What's next after I have created my first ever CV?**
It is essential to review your CV regularly, so that all new work experiences are included, reflecting an up-to-date account of your evidence against your chief skills. Remember, if you have completed a work placement add the proof, which may take the shape of a short description of what you did. Also don't forget to add new qualifications and exam results as you receive them.

■ **I feel big-headed if I write down my achievements and evidence: can you help?**
Are you one of those people who prefer not to think about all your achievements? Do you remember the negative experiences and push the positive experiences to one side? Often, individuals can be quite shy when it comes to selling their skills and experience. We don't like to appear big-headed. This *can* be a positive trait. However, when it comes to writing down all our experiences and transferable evidence you have to put this to one side and embrace your abilities, characteristics and transferable evidence.

■ **I have a disability and/or have had some difficult times at school/college – how do I include this in my CV?**
It is crucial that you record the information that makes you feel comfortable. It is also important to advise potential employers about certain things that they may need to know, for example, a physical adaptation they would need to provide.

It is not the easiest of tasks to find the right words to express this but it is important to decide and seek advice as to how this can be explained in your CV. It could be that you include it at the end of your CV, or you may wish to incorporate it into your profile, especially if it is a fundamental part of who you are.

Find ways of explaining and describing what this means for you, if you feel it's necessary. It does show your personal strength, resilience and many other positive traits, so make sure you seek feedback from another external party, if you think this will help (for example **Activity 1.2: Go with the flow**). Good employers will be impressed by people who have coped with a personal challenge or any difficulty; write it in a way that you feel expresses you fully.

Further Reading and Viewing

Patti Dobrowolski (2011) *Drawing Solutions: How Visual Goal Setting Will Change Your Life.* Creative Genius Press.

Susan Hodgson (2012) *The A–Z Careers and Jobs.* Kogan Page.

Elizabeth Holmes (2012) *What Next After School? All You Need to Know About Work, Travel and Study.* Kogan Page.

Kathleen Houston (2008) *You Want to do What?! Inspiring Ideas for an Alternative Career.* Trotmann.

Vanda North with Tony Buzan (2001) *Get Ahead – Mind Map Your Way to Success.* Buzan.

www.bbc.co.uk/skillswise
BBC Skillswise is a free-to-access website for adult numeracy and literacy tutors and students, with printable worksheets and factsheets and online games, videos and quizzes that can be used in class or by students at home.

www.careersbox.co.uk
Careersbox is a free online library of careers related film, news and information. As the preferred digital new media partner to the Institute of Career Guidance in the UK, Careersbox's aim is to deliver the right information at the right time to careers advisers and job seekers. They provide case study films showing real people doing real jobs, giving you insight into careers across all sectors and helping you to find the right career.

www.careerbuilder.co.uk
CareerBuilder has the largest online job site in the UK, but it's

more than just a job board. They provide useful hints and tips when compiling your CV and some great articles to help boost your profile.

www.careers4u.tv
An independent careers library, featuring interviews with young employees, apprentices and entrepreneurs who have been filmed in the workplace so you can see what their working life is really like. Their aim is to give you inspiration, spark ideas and, maybe, even help you decide what you don't want to do.

www.iCould.com
iCould is about inspiration and encouragement. The idea is to help you make the most of your potential and talent, by showing how others have used theirs. Profiling mini video films on real life people and their careers.

www.monster.co.uk
Monster.co.uk is the leading provider of online careers and recruitment resources, connecting candidates with hiring companies. If you're thinking about a new job, career, or direction, Monster can help you explore the possibilities and find the opportunities that are right for you. They also have a careers advice section, which is a one-stop guide to a wealth of information online, helping you with CVs, applications, interviews and salaries.

www.nationalcareersservice.direct.gov.uk
The National Careers Service is a new careers service available to young people and adults in England. The service will provide access to independent, professional guidance on careers, skills and the labour market.

www.wordle.net
Wordle is a toy for generating 'word clouds' from text that you provide. The clouds give greater prominence to words that appear more frequently in the source text. You can tweak your clouds with different fonts, layouts, and colour schemes. The images you create with Wordle are yours to use however you like. You can print them out, or save them to the Wordle gallery to share with your friends.

Appendix: Sample Interview Questions

1. What do you know about us/our company?

2. What sort of person would your friends say you are?

3. Why do you want to work here?

4. What qualities and/or experience do you have to offer our company?

5. What are your weaknesses?

6. What are your strengths?

7. Could you tell me about a project or task which you feel you have done particularly well?

8. What do you think makes a good team player? Tell me about any experience you have had working in a team.

9. Give me an example of when you have used your own initiative.

10. How would you cope with a difficult customer or diffuse a difficult situation?

About the Author

Having qualified as a person-centred Counsellor 18 years ago and with a degree in Health and 16+ Teacher's Certificate, Julia began teaching in Further and Higher Education as a Lecturer in Health and Social Care. She has worked in a variety of settings along the way – health promotion, education liaison, student recruitment for university, graduate employment – and since 2009 she has been developing her own writing, art and healing practice. Julia works one to one with clients, face to face and online, using a variety of tools and methods, written exercises and interactive activities that she has developed over the last 20 years, some of which you have been introduced to in this book. Her passion is writing and coaching others to realise their potential as well as integrating her art and healing practice into the mix. She is about to begin her third book and is working on developing creative online workshops and tutorials that will complement her two publications. Please visit www.juliadolowicz.com for more information and, if you'd like to read an informal bio and find out more about her art, please visit www.julesdollyart.co.uk

Index